Teaching information skills in schools

Teaching information skills in schools

James E. Herring

Acting Head, Department of Communication and Information Studies, Queen Margaret College, Edinburgh

LIBRARY ASSOCIATION PUBLISHING
LONDON

Published by
Library Association Publishing
7 Ridgmount Street
London WC1E 7AE

Library Association Publishing is wholly owned by The Library Association.

First published 1996

British Library Cataloguing in Publication Data
A catalogue record for this book is available from the British Library

ISBN 1-85604-176-X

Typeset in 11/13 Baskerville and Swiss 721 by Library Association Publishing.
Printed and made in Great Britain by Bookcraft (Bath) Ltd, Midsomer Norton, Avon.

This book is dedicated to the
memory of my brother, Bobby Herring
who died of cancer this year, aged 49
and to my friend Frank Lendrum
who died of cancer this year, aged 51

Contents

Acknowledgments

I would like to thank all the school librarians and teachers who sent me material for this book. I have not been able to use all of it but I hope that the selections made will be useful. In particular, I would like to thank the following people for their material and advice: Dorothy Williams, Mike McConnell, David Wray, Gaynor Long, Jim Ratter, Anne McIntosh, Michael Downie, Charlotte Macarthur, Duncan Grey, Sue Hurford, Eileen Armstrong, Fay Cooke, Fred Martin, Diane Swift, Morag Nicolson, Anthony Tilke, Bob Jones, Dennis Vickers and Mike Eisenberg.

Thanks also must go to Helen Carley and Lin Franklin at Library Association Publishing for their patience, advice and encouragement.

Finally, love and thanks to Val, Jonathan and Stuart who have put up with it all – again.

Figures 1.1 and 10.1 are reproduced by kind permission of Cassell Ltd. Figures 5.3, 5.7 and 8.5 are reproduced by kind permission of Lothian Regional Council.
Figure 8.1 is reproduced by kind permission of Hodder and Stoughton Ltd.
Figure 9.9 is reproduced by kind permission of Kogan Page Ltd.

Introduction: The PLUS model of information skills

The purpose of this book

In the mid-1980s, there was a flurry of research projects and books on information skills in schools and some reports have subsequently been published since then. The purpose of this book is to build on the work done in the mid 1980s since much of it is still very relevant in the late 1990s and to update the context of information skills in schools in the light of technological developments which have occurred in the 1990s. The book seeks to provide teachers and school librarians[1] with both a theoretical[2] context and practical examples of how they help pupils[2] to learn and use a range of cognitive skills when the pupils are involved in learning experiences which involve the use of information resources such as books, journals, CD-ROMs and the Internet. There is a need for a book such as this firstly, because in upper primary, in secondary schools and in further education, there is now a greater emphasis on project or assignment work which pupils and students are asked to complete within their academic subjects. Secondly, developments in information technology such as the greatly increased use of CD-ROMs in all schools and the growing availability of the Internet in schools has meant that pupils now have access to a much greater range and quantity of curriculum-related and relevant information resources than ever before. Even the smallest school library can now provide pupils with a huge amount of sources by purchasing a range of CD-ROMs, e.g. full text versions of national newspapers and by accessing the Internet. If this new technological advance is to be exploited effectively, then pupils will need guidance not only on how to access the material on CD-ROM or on the Internet (which they will find very easy) but also on how to select relevant information and ideas, reject information and ideas not relevant to their purpose, use appropriate reading and note taking strategies and restructure and manipulate information and ideas select-ed when presenting their work in the form of a written assignment or an oral or IT based presentation. Those involved in this task will there-fore need to be aware of research in the areas of learning, teaching, information skills, information technology, reading, writing and the management of school libraries. In the first four chapters, this book seeks to select key examples of this research and bring a range of theo-ries, concepts and practices together in order to focus on information skills which this author views as a range of interrelated skills which pupils need in order to learn more effectively in school. The second part of the book aims to relate the research covered in the first part to a series of practical examples from schools in the UK and other coun-tries so that teachers and school librarians can learn from their own pro-fessional colleagues by looking at examples of good practice which they may be able to adapt for their own school. Thus the purpose of the book is to combine theory and practice and to suggest a framework for teaching information skills.

Who should read this book?

The book's main focus is on secondary schools (age 11–18) but teachers and librarians in upper primary and secondary schools and in further education colleges can all benefit from the theory and practice available in this book. Parts of the book will appeal to different audiences to a greater or lesser extent although the book as a whole will be of interest to teachers and school librarians because of its up to date nature and the practical ideas included. The chapters on learning and teaching will be of particular interest to school librarians who may not have covered these areas in any depth in their undergraduate or postgraduate educa-tion but these chapters should also interest teachers who wish to refresh their knowledge in these areas. The chapter on information skills may contain much new material for teachers and will serve as a refresher course for school librarians. The chapter on whole school policies will be of interest to teachers, school librarians and senior management in schools and colleges as it demonstrates the need for cooperation between professional colleagues in schools in the area of information skills. The subsequent chapters on aspects of information skills can be used by teachers and school librarians together to form the basis of an integrated programme for their school. The examples provided and the teaching plans included in these chapters are not to be viewed as prescriptive but more as starting points for discussion amongst teachers and school librarians.

The book will also be of interest to those involved in teaching trainee teachers and librarians and to the students on undergraduate and postgraduate courses in teaching, information management and library and information studies.

The PLUS model

The PLUS model proposed in this book seeks to provide a framework for teachers and school librarians which they can use with pupils when introducing aspects of information skills. The model covers:

✔ **P**urpose – identifying the purpose of an investigation or assignment
✔ **L**ocation – finding relevant information resources related to the purpose
✔ **U**se – selecting and rejecting information and ideas, reading for information, note taking and presentation
✔ **S**elf-evaluation – how pupils evaluate their performance in applying information skills to the assignment and what they learn for the future.

The intention here is not to suggest that the PLUS model is radically different from other models noted in this book but to provide staff in schools with an integrated framework, with a positive acronym, which can be used by both pupils and those who teach and support them. Allowing pupils to focus on their own learning processes, with guidance from teachers and school librarians, by using the PLUS model will help pupils to think more clearly about what skills they should be using when asked to demonstrate what they have learned in particular subject areas by completing projects or assignments. The PLUS model is a *suggested* framework which individual schools may wish to adapt to their own needs when working with pupils.

References

1 The term 'school librarian' is used throughout this book as it is the term used to represent professional librarians working in secondary schools in the UK. Many schools in the UK still do not have full time school librarians but this book will be very relevant to those teachers in charge of school libraries in such schools. The term will also cover library media specialists in the USA and teacher librarians in Canada and Australia.

2 The term 'pupil' is used throughout this book as many schools in the UK use this term to cover those attending school. The author recognizes that some UK schools refer to pupils as students and that this term is common in other countries. The author does not regard the term 'pupil' as in any way demeaning to those who attend school.

Chapter 1
Learning

After reading this chapter, you will be able to:

✔ **critically examine a range of definitions of learning**
✔ **evaluate a range of learning theories**
✔ **understand the importance of intelligence and memory in pupils' learning**
✔ **understand how pupils develop individual learning styles**
✔ **evaluate a range of learning strategies which can be used to enhance learning in the classroom and in the school library**
✔ **understand the effect of different teaching methods on pupils' learning.**

In order to teach pupils how to learn and practice effective information skills, teachers and school librarians will be helped by increasing their understanding of how pupils learn and the complex factors involved in learning. This chapter may be more useful to school librarians whose education has not necessarily involved the study of education, but teachers may usefully use this chapter to update themselves on some of the many debates surrounding the subject of learning. The existing literature on learning shows that despite a massive amount of research over the past 50 years, there remains no exact agreement amongst researchers on several aspects of learning. For example, it is agreed that each individual learns differently but there is no agreement as to why this should be so. This chapter does not seek to provide a comprehensive overview of all aspects of learning theory and research currently available but will focus on what aspects of learning teachers and school librarians might use as the basis for teaching information skills, as many writers provide valuable insights into what assumptions may be made about pupils' learning and, as importantly, what assumptions should be avoided. To achieve this end this chapter will examine definitions of learning; learning theories; aspects of intelligence, memory and thinking; learning styles; learning strategies and how teaching methods and styles can help or hinder learning in the classroom and in the school library.

Definitions of learning

Hohn argues that while no single definition of learning is accepted, 'Most argue that learning involves the acquisition of new elements of knowledge, skills, beliefs, feelings and specific behaviours as well as changes in existing elements'[1] and that 'Learning involves either a change in behaviours or the capacity to change one's behaviour in the future'.[2]

That is, a person can be said to have learned something if it can be shown that s/he can understand, explain or do something which s/he could not do previously. Learning must be separated from development which may be attributable solely to growth. For example, almost all children 'learn' how to walk but the ability to walk derives from physical development and not from understanding of the process of walking. Thus 'learning' to walk should not be seen in the same light as learning done later in a pupil's life in secondary school, e.g. learning about the origins of World War 2.

Learning is a very complex subject and what influences learning directly or indirectly affects any attempt at defining learning. Most writers on the topic agree that in schools, a pupil's existing knowledge is a key factor in learning in that pupils build on what they know when learning new topics. However, Cullingford points out that 'Learning is both constant and changeable; it depends on moods and general attitudes; it changes according to emotions and yet is a constant base on which other matters depend'.[3]

Thus the fact that pupils *have* existing knowledge does not necessarily mean that they will reflect on or actively use that knowledge when learning something new.

A second key aspect which influences learning is, according to Howe, what the pupil does when learning something new in school.

This 'doing' takes many forms in secondary schools, from listening to the teacher, to reading, to experimenting in science or using a CD-ROM in the school library. When pupils are carrying out such activities, Howe argues that 'Information that is perceived by the learner is subjected to cognitive activity that results in a modification of the individual's capacities: something new has been learned'.[4]

In schools, a third influencing factor on pupils' learning is the teacher and the methods employed in order to create a good environment for learning. Whitaker argues that 'Teachers can build creative mentoring partnerships to ensure sustained educational growth and development'.[5]

Howe reinforces this point, stating that the key role of the teacher can be to help pupils recognize the existing knowledge which they have and encourage pupils to develop ways of using this knowledge creatively.[6] In relation to teaching information skills, this is a key point and later in this book there will be an examination of what teachers and school librarians can do to help pupils learn effectively.

Lastly, it is generally agreed that individuals learn differently from one another and apply different learning methods at different times. This provides obvious difficulties for teachers and school librarians who often teach pupils in groups. One way to counteract this difficulty is to encourage pupils themselves to examine the way they learn and the section on learning strategies below will explore this further.

Thus attempts at defining learning can be useful in that such attempts can provide teachers and school librarians with a challenge: to identify more clearly what pupils are to learn, how they might learn, what factors will influence this learning and how this learning can be measured. As Hohn notes, 'Learning is a process, the existence of which we infer from changes in performance and there must be criteria or standards against which this learning is measured'.[7]

Learning theories

There have been numerous theories of learning in the twentieth century and, as with definitions of learning above, no single theory is accepted by educational psychologists who have done research in this area. It is not the purpose of this book to examine the range of learning theories in detail, but by briefly looking at the main aspects of the major theoretical schools of learning, teachers and school librarians will be provided with a theoretical base for teaching information skills and also methods of taking a critical view of suggested programmes for teaching such skills in secondary schools.

Both Entwistle and Hohn provide useful outlines of how learning theories have been proposed, criticized and developed over the past 40 years and what aspects of the different theoretical models have influenced their own models of learning in schools.

Behaviourist theories

In the 1960s, the behaviourist theories dominated the educational scene, heavily influenced by the work of Skinner and Bloom. The behaviourist approach, many elements of which are still very influential in the 1990s, established a series of principles for learning based mainly on the stimulus-response theory. The first principle to be established was contiguity. It was argued that when a stimulus is closely followed by a response and this is repeated, then the response may become automatic, i.e. the person will learn how to respond. Thus repetition, the second principle, was seen as very important if learning was to take place. The third principle, the law of effect, is based on the fact that where reinforcement takes place – often in the shape of approval or offers of reward – learning will be enhanced.[8]

According to Entwistle, Skinner's work with animals was transferred to the educational setting and Skinner argued that learning depended on three major elements:

1 Dividing the learning requirement into a series of small stages and producing a logical sequence of events.
2 Providing rewards for correct responses at each stage and reinforcing the stages from time to time.
3 Examining the existing behaviour and using reinforcement until new patterns of behaviour had been learned.[9]

When these principles were related to learning in schools, Skinner's view was that teachers did not provide enough reinforcement for pupils and that this restricted learning possibilities. The development of programmed learning tried to put Skinner's theories into practice in schools but by the 1970s, it was argued that while some elements of Skinner's theories were acceptable, they were not generally applicable. Entwistle cites McKeachie as arguing that learning in schools cannot always be seen as a series of steps to be completed because 'meaningful educational learning is both more robust and more complex ... This complexity, so frustrating to those who wish to proscribe educational methods, is a reminder of the fascinating uniqueness of the learner'. In a final comment on Skinner's theories, Entwistle states that 'The learning we require of pupils is not the unconscious link between stimulus and response but the acquisition of knowledge and skills which can be used reflectively and applied effectively in subsequent education and in later life'.[10]

In relation to teaching information skills, teachers and school librarians can learn from aspects of Skinner's work. For example, it will be helpful to explain to pupils that by following a series of stages in project work, they should achieve better organized and knowledge-based work which will meet the demands of the task in hand. What cannot be argued is that all pupils will produce well researched and logically structured projects merely by following a number of steps. As Entwistle notes, Skinner's theories are 'too simplistic to explain a wide range of human behaviour in social settings and too mechanistic to incorporate the individuality of human response to stimuli'.[11]

The complexity of learning

Subsequent theories of learning have developed a number of themes and assumptions in the behaviourist models. The key differences in models of learning in the 1980s and 1990s have been the recognition of the complexity of learning and the large number of factors which affect an individual's learning. Thus the work of Bruner and Ausubel on information processing theories; of Gardner and Eysenck on learning in relation to individual differences, e.g. personality; of Cronbach and Entwistle on interactionist theories of learning; and Kolb and Morton on experiential learning identify the multiplicity of influences on the learning done by pupils in secondary schools.[12] Teachers and school librarians will develop their own preferences as to which model or mixture of models of learning they wish to follow but it is important that they adopt a stance which allows for different models to be taken into consideration when dealing with the individual approaches taken by some pupils which might not fit in with the methods used by the majority of pupils in a class.

Intelligence and memory

A major concern of researchers and writers on learning has been to try to understand how the mind works and how pupils use their minds to learn new ideas or skills. The term 'intelligence' is widely used in education but there is little agreement as to its meaning. In schools, pupils may be branded as 'bright', 'intelligent', 'not very bright', or 'unintelligent' if they succeed or fail in producing work which meets the demands of the task set by the teacher. Entwistle states that individual differences in learning amongst pupils are often directly related to concepts of intelligence but he argues that a pupil's intelligence can be affected by inheritance as well as by social and environmental factors. Entwistle cites Gardner's theories of intelligence as being related to problem solving abilities in which the pupil uses intelligence to create something new (i.e. to learn) from a problem. Gardner's ideas on aspects of intelligence such as linguistic and spatial are criticized by Entwistle as being too speculative.[13]

Whitaker argues that intelligence should not just be seen as being linked to cognitive abilities such as problem solving and cites Handy who argues that several types of intelligence exist, including practical, analytical, linguistic, spatial, musical, physical, intuitive and interpersonal and it is the mix of such intelligences which are important in how pupils learn. These types of intelligence should cover social and emotional aspects of learning, Whitaker argues, as well as cognitive aspects.[14]

Thinking skills are seen as important to the learning process and these skills are related to how pupils store, analyse and retrieve information, ideas and concepts when learning. Entwistle states that each individual has a range of 'schemata' which are used to relate new perceptions to existing perceptions when learning. For example, if pupils are learning about climatic changes in geography, they will relate their existing knowledge about the earth's structure and climate to new perceptions, e.g. global warming, in order to understand the effect of global warming on the earth's climate. If the pupils fail to understand this new concept, then other information may be needed because either existing knowledge is lacking or that knowledge cannot be remembered in a usable form.[15]

Claxton gives an excellent overview of how memory and the mind can be seen in different ways according to the model used. For example, Claxton states that the way individuals use their short term and long term memories is often seen as similar to the way a computer stores information. However, this analogy is only partly useful as pupils will store and retrieve information in ways which do not follow the logical sequencing of information in a computer. Claxton also gives examples of the mind as a switchboard or a library. According to Claxton, the key developments in the study of the mind in recent times 'include seeing knowledge as more integrated, less atomistic; more fine-grained and fuzzy, less clearly definable and molar; more mutable and provisional, less rigid and objective; more situation specific, less general purpose; more process and content together, less separation between knowing how and knowing that'.[16]

When teaching information skills, it will thus be necessary to realize the range of factors which will affect how pupils use their existing knowledge when approaching learning tasks. The ability of pupils to remember concepts or facts will be influenced by how much attention was paid when these concepts were explained or these facts written down. Therefore, teaching pupils about the process of learning and the importance of noting key aspects when reading texts will enable some pupils to use their memories and 'intelligence' to good effect.

Learning styles

Hohn states that pupils' learning styles refer to 'beliefs, preferences and behaviours used by individuals to aid their learning in a given situation'.[17] There are different types of learning styles, including cognitive styles which relate to how pupils perceive what is being taught or what they are reading, how they remember concepts, information and skills, how they think about what they are doing in the classroom or school library and how they solve problems. Physiological styles relate to the pupils' preferred environment, e.g. where they prefer to study and affective styles relate to their personality and individual preferences, e.g. whether they enjoy studying alone or in a group, in silence or with background noise. Learning styles are to some extent different for each individual and while teachers can use tests to identify individual learning styles, Hohn argues that 'it is impractical to try to construct enough adaptations to meet each possible learning style effectively'.[18]

Entwistle argues that pupils will all be different in their preferred uses of memory with some pupils preferring to use convergent or divergent thinking although everyone is capable of both types. Entwistle warns against using extremes when discussing learning styles, stating that teachers should not classify pupils either as having convergent or divergent styles as pupils will often adapt their styles in different situations. Learning styles relate to the use of different parts of the brain with the left hemisphere being used mainly for what Entwistle describes as 'linguistic, symbolic and semantic schemata, for conscious internal memorising and for logical, sequential or analytic reasoning'.[19] Schools tend to concentrate too much on pupils developing left hemisphere based styles, Entwistle states, despite the fact that right hemisphere influenced styles allow pupils to more easily use visual memory and adopt more holistic approaches to problems which teachers recognize as being characteristic of successful pupils.[20]

Whitaker argues that learning styles should be linked with learning stances in that pupils will adopt different behaviours with different teachers or in different subject areas. Thus the same pupil can be attention seeking and work haphazardly in one situation and very attentive and consistently hard working in others. What pupils are trying to do, Whitaker states, is work out what is being asked of them and how they can use their existing knowledge and skills in a new learning situation. Whitaker cites the work of Honey and Mumford on learning styles which develop from pupils' preferences in feeling, watching, thinking and doing both in school and elsewhere. Learning styles can be categorized in different ways and Honey and Mumford's views of learning styles include the reflector who is able to reflect on concrete experiences and draw conclusions from the experience; the theorist who is able to reflect on information available in different forms and can develop ideas from this; the pragmatist who is able to examine problems and think about a range of solutions; and the activist who is able to experiment with new ideas, view learning as a challenge and take risks in dealing with different learning tasks.[21]

Learning styles and information skills

In teaching information skills, teachers and school librarians will need to be conscious of the existence of a range of learning styles amongst pupils and also of the fact that pupils in the early years of secondary school (aged 12–14) will still be developing their learning styles. Most writers on learning styles agree that pupils should be able to progress from serialist styles, in which pupils look at individual aspects of a topic in turn, to holistic styles through which pupils can explore the topic as a whole and understand the interrelationship of different aspects of the topic. Learning styles reflect a complex mix of individual traits and preferences of pupils and are affected by a number of factors such as classroom environment, the home, the teacher and the pupils' peers. Thus teachers and school librarians can help pupils to examine their own learning by developing in them an awareness of the importance of reflection in the work they do in schools.

Learning strategies

Howe states that, 'No educational objective is more important than learning to learn and how to function as an independent, autonomous learner',[22] and that learning should not be seen merely in the context of the school but as a lifelong experience. Pupils need to acquire a set of tools for learning, Howe states, and these tools may 'take the form of learning strategies and techniques. The good learner has acquired a large repertoire of such techniques and knows how to use them effectively, how to choose the most appropriate technique for a particular task, when to apply particular methods and how to adapt them for new uses'.[23]

Whitaker argues that there is a need for pupils to develop a set of learning strategies in his version of experiential learning. Whitaker's model examines how pupils learn through experience and can be encouraged to reflect on these experiences, which enables them to make decisions about what learning strategies are needed in different circumstances, e.g. listening to a teacher's explanation or watching a video in class. Whitaker distinguishes between deliberate experiential learning and incidental experiential learning. In the deliberate route, pupils will be encouraged, for example, to reflect on work done for a curriculum-related project, draw conclusions from this (e.g. the need to

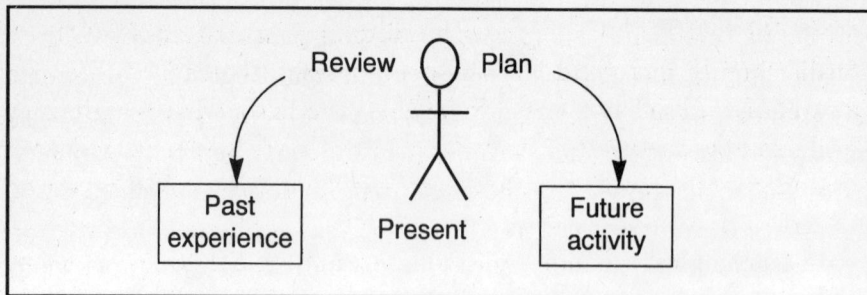

Fig. 1.1 *Whitaker's deliberate learning route*

have a better plan), examine new/better methods of doing a similar project and putting this into practice when planning a new project. In the incidental route, pupils go from one project to another without reflecting on what they might have done to improve their own work. Whitaker argues that in the deliberate learning route 'this iterative process of action, reflection and planning is at the heart of all successful learning'.[24]

Figure 1.1 shows how Whitaker's deliberate learning route can allow pupils the opportunity to improve their learning by reflection.

Good learners

Claxton argues that what he terms 'good learners' have developed a range of learning strategies which allow them to cope with different kinds of learning challenges. These learners have good attitudes to learning and are 'oriented towards seeing and seizing learning opportunities when they are congruent with the learner's own priorities and interests'.[25] Such pupils are also resilient when faced with difficulties in learning and are able to cope with any feelings of uncertainty about their initial understanding of a topic. Good learners have the ability to judge what learning routes to follow, have a realistic view of what they can achieve and an idea of what resources are available to them. In schools, such pupils have a range of strategies which enable them to gather relevant information in different ways. According to Claxton, these pupils have key learning strengths which include the ability to ask questions of material with which they work and seek suitable answers using different methods, e.g. reading, listening, experimenting. Claxton further argues that good learners need 'insight: the capacity for clear awareness and self awareness, to be able to monitor what is happening, evaluate how the strategy is working, assess when to persist and when to adjust and reapplies priorities in the light of developing experience.'[26]

In teaching information skills, teachers and school librarians will be aware that not all pupils will meet the criteria of Claxton's 'good learners' and that factors such as motivation, maturity, personality, home environment and peer relationships may influence the pupils' capacity or willingness to apply learning strategies in school. However, it is clearly one of the aims of teaching information skills to provide pupils with access to the skills and abilities of good learners by explaining some of the strategies open to pupils when learning. Such strategies will include planning skills, listening skills, reading skills, viewing skills, note taking skills, summarizing skills, writing skills, presentation skills and reflective skills and the second half of this book will explore methods of giving pupils opportunities to acquire such skills and apply them, as appropriate, across the curriculum.

Concept maps

A number of writers on learning refer to the use of concept maps as a constructive strategy which pupils can use to increase their understanding of aspects of a concept or topic. Whitaker states that as psychologists understand more about how the two sides of the brain work, it is clear that not all learners think in a linear fashion and that some learners employ a range of methods such as word association, visual memory and existing experience when learning new concepts or topics. Whitaker cites the work of Buzan who encouraged teachers to explore topics by using mindmaps which place the topic at the centre of the page and pupils make a map by identifying key aspects of that topic. Whitaker also refers to methods in which pupils create diagrams not only with words but by using visual images, sometimes using colour. The use of such maps will, Whitaker argues, allow a more spontaneous approach to learning than traditional listing techniques and will help pupils to 'create their own classification . . . as a means of extending the mind in its struggle for insight and understanding'.[27]

Entwistle refers to the work of Novak who urged teachers to use concept maps to enable pupils to see the connections between different concepts. Concept mapping can help pupils to use visual images and to understand how links are made between concepts. This is different from rote learning in which pupils may only remember aspects of a topic but not how these aspects are linked together.[28]

Teaching styles and learning

Chapter 3 will examine in some detail the range of teaching methods open to teachers and school librarians when teaching information skills but all researchers on learning in schools agree that one of the many influences on pupils' ability or willingness to learn is the teaching style adopted by the teacher and the learning environment in which pupils work. Whitaker, amongst others, notes that while pupils are legally obliged to attend school, they must volunteer to learn. The role of the teacher and the school librarian is to provide the environment which will, Whitaker argues, encourage pupils to define their own ambitions; provide pupils with 'emotional and psychological encouragement'; allow pupils to talk to each other and to their teachers about their learning and how to recognize their skills and abilities; and ensure that pupils reflect on their own learning.[29] Howe argues that teaching styles do influence learning but indirectly in that teachers can help pupils to recognize existing knowledge or help the pupil to use a range of activities which will encourage learning.[30] Entwistle states that teaching styles are one factor in his heuristic model of learning and that teachers influence learning but are not the determining factor in pupils' learning. Entwistle puts teaching methods in context by arguing that the key influences on learning are 'skill in learning, attitude to education, approach to learning, learning tasks, knowledge base and skill in teaching'.[31]

Conclusion

As was stated at the beginning of this chapter, there is no agreement amongst researchers on key aspects of how and why pupils learn or do not learn effectively in schools. Teachers and school librarians will, therefore, attempt to take account of a wide range of factors when trying to increase the learning capabilities of pupils in teaching information skills in the classroom and in the school library. The key issue to arise in this brief overview of learning, is that of the importance of how pupils relate their existing knowledge and skills to the acquisition of new knowledge and skills. In enabling pupils to 'learn how to learn' teachers and school librarians are faced with the difficulty of asking relatively young children (e.g. aged 12) to reflect on their own learning style and to build up a portfolio of abilities to allow them to acquire a range of skills in thinking, reasoning, judging, deciding and evaluating. This task is not made easier by the difficulty of such concepts and the often complicated language used to describe them.

As was seen with the criticism of behaviourism, teaching pupils to learn is not achieved merely by identifying a number of steps to be followed on every occasion. For example, teaching pupils to use intonation in speaking French and teaching pupils about the relationship between the heart and other organs of the body will make different demands on the learning approaches and abilities of pupils. Thus while it is possible to identify key aspects of teaching information skills: purpose, location, use and self-evaluation, there is no guarantee that all pupils will approach such skills in the same way. Teachers and school librarians themselves can learn to identify the factors affecting learning such as pupils' self esteem, the learning environment and the pupils' existing knowledge and skills and try to allow individual pupils to improve their own approaches to learning by appreciating the benefits of implementing the information skills taught by teachers and school librarians.

References

1   Hohn, R., *Classroom learning and teaching*, Longman USA, 1995.
2   ibid.
3   Cullingford, C., *Children, teachers and learning*, Cassell, 1990.
4   Howe, M., *A teacher's guide to the psychology of learning*, Blackwell, 1984.
5   Whitaker, P., *Managing to learn*, Cassell, 1995.
6   Howe, M., op cit.
7   Hohn, R., op. cit.
8   Entwistle, N., *Understanding classroom learning*, Hodder and Stoughton, 1987.
9   ibid.

10 ibid.

11 ibid.

12 See Hohn, R., op. cit. for a review of these theories.

13 Entwistle, N., op. cit.

14 Whitaker, P., op. cit.

15 Entwistle, N., op. cit.

16 Claxton, G., *Teaching to learn*, Cassell, 1990.

17 Hohn, R., op. cit.

18 ibid.

19 Entwistle, N., op. cit.

20 ibid.

21 Honey, P. and Mumford, A., *Manual of learning styles*, P Honey, 1986.

22 Howe, M., op. cit.

23 ibid.

24 Whitaker, P., op. cit.

25 Claxton, G., op. cit.

26 ibid.

27 Whitaker, P., op. cit.

28 Entwistle, N., op. cit.

29 Whitaker, P., op. cit.

30 Howe, M., op. cit.

31 Entwistle, N., op. cit.

Chapter 2
Information skills

After reading this chapter, you will be able to:

✔ **evaluate a range of definitions of information skills**
✔ **understand the interrelated nature of information skills in the PLUS model**
✔ **appreciate the implications of IT developments for information skills teaching in schools**
✔ **learn new approaches to information skills, including evaluation.**

There is already a vast literature on information skills which is available to teachers and school librarians. This chapter seeks to select some of the key readings from that literature and provide an overview of a number of aspects of information skills which will be expanded upon in later chapters. Much of the literature on information skills has concentrated too much on skills related to use of the library without providing a proper learning context for these skills. In this chapter, the focus will be on the need for pupils to integrate a range of skills to identify the purpose of, locate and use concepts, ideas and information in whatever form they exist. The debate on information skills is a global debate and reference will be made to work done in a number of different countries but it is important to note that, irrespective of which country material may come from, there is agreement that information skills are learning skills and that teachers and school librarians who teach such skills should concentrate on the cognitive aspects of information used by pupils and not merely on the mechanical skills involved in finding information from books, journals and CD-ROMs.

This chapter will examine some definitions of information skills, the interrelationship of a number of related skills, the implications of IT in schools for information skills development, and approaches to teaching information skills including evaluation.

Definitions

The terms 'information skills' and 'study skills' have been used in schools across the world to cover a wide range of skills which pupils use when working on individual or group work which at some point involves pupils in using information resources and producing written work which is assessed by a teacher. In some cases, there has been a tendency for 'information skills' to be related mainly to pupils' use of libraries in schools or elsewhere and for 'study skills' to relate to pupils classroom work or to revision for coursework or examinations. Such distinctions are not helpful as they attempt to categorize a range of skills which are interrelated and which pupils use at varying stages of school work. Information skills are seen by this author as the skills which pupils use to identify the purpose of, locate, process and communicate information, concepts and ideas and then reflect on the effective application of these skills. Irving states that the term 'information skills' is 'a broad term incorporating a range of subordinate or prerequisite skills; those associated with reading, writing, searching, retrieving, organising, processing, thinking, analysing and presenting',[1] and argues that the term 'information skills' is less exclusive than 'library skills' or 'study skills' in that it relates to what pupils do in schools but also to pupils' use of information resources outside school and in their future working lives. Earlier, Marland defined information skills as covering areas such as 'library-user education, reading development, experimental and research training, study skills and media literacy'.[2] If writing today, Marland would have included the use of IT-based information sources in his definition. Wray and Lewis accept that the term 'information skills' is a useful one to cover an array of skills but they argue that using terms such as 'information skills' or 'reading for information', 'tends to indicate a separation of these ways of interacting with texts from ways more generally referred to as "reading"'.[3]

Rogers, reviewing research in this area, cites Hopkins as arguing that, 'There is an unresolved dichotomy and confusion between the notion of information skills as (a) the retrieval and location of information and (b) the analysis and synthesis of information. The former aspect of the term is most commonly the focus of information skills programmes but the latter is arguably the most important'.4

Rogers also refers to the work of Thomson and Meek who argue that the key focus of information skills teaching should be on the extent to which the use of information resources enhances understanding amongst pupils and that information skills must be taught as part of the curriculum, not as a separate set of skills.5 Brown argues that information skills should be seen in the context of learning as, 'Numerous studies and reports which analyse and evaluate our approaches to the learning process identify the need for students to develop independent learning skills as a key factor for success.'6

Wray defines information skills as 'all the skills necessary for pupils successfully to cope with the information environment in which they find themselves, be this in or out of school' and argues that teaching information skills in schools needs to be done in relation to different approaches which include aspects of finding relevant resources, 'linking the use of libraries to the wider skills of reading, asking questions, taking notes and generally using the tools of self directed learning' and relating information skills to social as well as educational needs.7

Interrelated skills

A number of studies over the past 15 years have sought to identify the key aspects of information skills by producing lists of interrelated skills which pupils will be expected to use when completing assignments of different kinds in schools. These lists are worth examining in order to identify both the similarities and the differences in emphasis of the authors. There is inevitably much overlap between the range of information skills outlines shown below and teachers and school librarians may wish to examine these lists in relation to their own school curriculum and choose elements from the lists which provide a best fit for their own school. Much of the work done in compiling such lists was done in the 1980s before the real impact of IT in schools and school libraries but the skills identified relate to school curricula in which pupils use 'traditional' information sources as well as those which increasingly provide pupils with access to an array of electronic sources of information.

The range of skills included in the term 'information skills' in this book covers the broad areas of purpose, location, use and self-evaluation which make up the PLUS model of information skills and these skills include:

Purpose
✔ cognitive skills in identifying existing knowledge
✔ thinking skills such as brainstorming or concept mapping
✔ skills in identifying information resources.

Location
✔ locational skills such as the ability to find information in library catalogues, books, journals, CD-ROMs and online information sources
✔ selection skills in assessing the relevance of information resources
✔ IT skills in using electronic sources such as the Internet.

Use
✔ reading skills including the ability to skim and scan information resources to find relevant information or ideas
✔ interactive skills including the ability to understand the content of what is being read, viewed or listened to and the ability to relate this to existing knowledge
✔ selective skills including the ability to select the appropriate information and to reject irrelevant information in the context of the purpose identified for using a particular information resource
✔ evaluation skills including the ability to evaluate information and ideas in relation to aspects such as the currency of the information or ideas, the author and any possible bias in the text
✔ recording skills including the ability to take notes in a systematic way which relates to understanding and purpose
✔ synthesizing skills including the ability to bring together related ideas, facts and information about a topic and relating this to existing knowledge
✔ writing or presentational skills including the ability to write an essay or report or project in a well structured, logically ordered manner which uses the information and ideas found to good effect.

Self-evaluation

✔ self-evaluation skills including the ability to reflect on the processes involved in assignment-related work and to identify areas of improvement in the effective use of information resources in the future.

Of these skills, the most important in terms of pupils' learning are those cognitive skills used by pupils when thinking about purpose, reading, evaluating, synthesizing, writing and reflecting. The skills involved in actually finding resources whether print or otherwise, whether in the library or elsewhere, are very necessary skills but are not as important as the other skills identified above and it is a major criticism of schools and school librarians in particular, that they have concentrated too much time and effort on finding skills and too little on cognitive skills.

Marland's model

The starting point for most information skills work in the UK remains the nine-step plan identified by Marland's group in 1981 which tried to identify a number of questions which pupils could ask themselves when doing assignments in school and accompanied these questions with statements for teachers and school librarians which identified skills in relation to each question. Figure 2.1 shows the nine questions and statements.

Question	Statement
1. What do I need to do?	formulate and analyse need
2. Where could I go?	identify and appraise likely sources
3. How do I get to the information?	locate individual resources
4. Which resources shall I use?	examine, select and reject individual resources
5. How shall I use the resources?	interrogate resources
6. What should I make a record of ?	record and store information
7. Have I got the information I need?	interpret, analyse, synthesize, evaluate
8. How should I present it?	present, communicate
9. What have I achieved?	evaluate

Fig. 2.1 Marland's model of information skills

It was not Marland's intention that the list of skills should be proscriptive in each school nor that pupils would need to follow *all* the steps for every project they did. Marland argued that the steps represented a logical sequence but pupils might have to retrace some of the steps, depending on the success of their approach. Marland also stressed that the nine steps were not discrete but had to be seen as an interrelated sequence of steps to guide pupils.[8] Marland's list of skills (and other similar lists) can inevitably be criticized because they represent generalizations and as Tabberer notes 'the way each category hides so many subskills (and skills of such very different kinds) ranging from high order reading skills to simple organisational skills'.[9]

The EXIT model

Wray and Lewis praise Marland's nine steps for the way in which they encourage pupils to think about their own learning, in that, 'Pupils are, therefore, encouraged to take a more metacognitive stance on their own activities'.

Wray and Lewis produce their own version of Marland's steps by identifying a series of ten stages which can be accompanied by questions for the pupils to ask themselves. Wray and Lewis refer to these stages as the EXIT (Extending Interactions with Texts) model. Figure 2.2 outlines the stages and questions posed by Wray and Lewis.[10]

Wray and Lewis acknowledge the difficulty of 'representing a complex and essentially recursive set of processes in the two-dimensional space defined by print on paper' and note that the use of numerical stages is merely a convenient method to use. Wray and Lewis's model clearly puts more emphasis than other models on reading and they argue that the processes involved should be seen as 'one of transaction, that is, the active construction of meaning in negotiation with the text as written'.[11]

The work of Wray and Lewis is a valuable contribution to research on information skills and raises a number of important questions for teachers and school librarians in relation to the emphasis they put on reading strategies for secondary school pupils. While Wray and Lewis's work is based in primary schools, it should not be assumed by secondary school teachers and school librarians that all pupils will necessarily have acquired the necessary sophistication in reading which they will need when faced with difficult texts in print or in electronic form.

Process stages	Questions
1 Elicitation of previous knowledge	1. What do I already know about this subject?
2 Establishing purposes	2. What do I need to find out and what will I do with the information?
3 Locating information	3. Where and how will I get this information?
4 Adopting an appropriate strategy	4. How shall I use this source of information to get what I need?
5 Interacting with text	5. What can I do to help me understand this better?
6 Monitoring understanding	6. What can I do if there are parts I cannot understand?
7 Making a record	7. What should I make a note of from this information?
8 Evaluating information	8. Which items of information should I believe and which should I keep an open mind about?
9 Assisting memory	9. How can I help myself remember the important parts?
10 Communicating information	10. How should I let other people know about this?

Fig. 2.2 *Wray and Lewis's model*

The Big Six model

In the United States, the work done by Eisenberg and Berkovitz is the one most often cited in the literature relating to information skills. Their approach to information skills is referred to as the 'Big Six Skills' which are defined as 'a systematic approach to information problem solving; six broad skill areas necessary for successful information problem solving; and a complete library and information skills curriculum'.

The six skills which are identified by Eisenberg and Berkovitz are:

1 Task definition – determine exactly what the information problem is and determine the specific information needs related to the problem.

2 Information seeking strategies – once the problem is clearly articulated, attention turns to the range of possible information sources [and] . . . selecting sources appropriate to the defined task.
3 Location and access – once students have decided on the appropriate strategy, this strategy must be carried out . . . Examples include: use of access tools, arrangement of materials, parts of a book and strategies for searching an online catalog.
4 Use of information – once students are able to locate and access a source, they must be able to read, view, listen or interact with the information and decide what is valuable for their particular situation.
5 Synthesis – is the restructuring or repackaging of information into new or different formats to meet the requirements of the task.
6 Evaluation – determines how effectively and efficiently the information problem solving process was conducted.[12]

The NCET model

Brown cites work done by the National Council for Educational Technology (NCET) which produced a list of questions for pupils doing assignments which involve the use of information resources of various kinds. The NCET's questions are:

1 Do I understand what I have to do?
2 Do I know where to find information?
3 Which skills will help me find what I really need?
4 How can I make sense of what I have found?
5 How do I know what to throw away?
6 Do I understand the information I have decided to use?
7 How should I present what I have found?
8 How can I show how much research I have done?

Brown argues that by allowing pupils to explore the processes involved in doing assignments, there will emerge benefits to both pupils and teachers and states that, 'Encouraging good research habits in students can considerably improve the quality of their research'.[13]

Irving's model

Irving, who was very influential in the formation of Marland's nine steps, produced her own nine steps which consisted of:

1 Defining tasks
2 Considering sources
3 Finding resources
4 Making selections
5 Effective use
6 Making records
7 Making sense
8 Presenting work
9 Assessing progress.

Irving argues that it is very important for teachers and school librarians to examine information skills from the pupils' point of view and not the teacher's and that information skills should relate to 'the continuous thread of assignments which form a substantial part of a pupil's school life'.

Irving also states that the nine steps are not a sequence which must be followed by every pupil doing an assignment and that, in some cases, some of the steps will need to be repeated if pupils run into difficulties, e.g. if pupils cannot find sufficient resources or do not fully understand the content of sources found. The steps are therefore valuable to both teachers and pupils as pupils can use the steps to monitor their own progress during assignments and teachers can use the steps to gauge whether pupils need extra help at some stage.[14]

Tabberer's model

As with Irving's book, the work done by Tabberer in the late 1980s is still very relevant today. Tabberer classifies information skills into areas of activity by the pupil and identifies the following categories:

✔ planning, including brainstorming and concept mapping
✔ finding information, including knowledge of the existence of, access to and appropriateness of information resources

✔ using information, including reading strategies, selection and rejection of information and note taking
✔ presenting information, including writing
✔ reviewing, including reflection and evaluation of performance.

Tabberer argues that teachers can profitably use information skills as a basis for planning the curriculum as 'it can be argued that any term's work should be judged by (amongst other things) the opportunity it gives students to practise and learn each group of skills'.[15]

An Australian model

In Australia, the Australian School Library Association is producing a multimedia, interactive CD-ROM entitled 'Teaching information skills'. The aim of the CD-ROM is to provide an opportunity for teachers and school librarians to enhance their understanding of the information process in schools and to develop their confidence and competency in teaching information skills across the curriculum. The information processing framework used has been developed nationally and takes the form of:

✔ defining
✔ locating
✔ selecting
✔ creating/presenting
✔ evaluating.

The 'evaluating' refers to how the pupils reflect on their own work but evaluation is seen as a key skill throughout the process, i.e. pupils will need to evaluate the extent to which they have effectively defined the task in hand.[16]

Review of models

This review of a variety of attempts to classify the key aspects of information skills demonstrates a number of key issues which need to be considered by teachers and school librarians who are planning information skills programmes in their own schools. Firstly, there is agreement amongst researchers that information skills must be regarded as a number of interrelated skills which should not be isolated from each other in the pupils' minds and that pupils should be encouraged to view the process as a whole as well as examining individual skills. Thus pupils who are reading or viewing or listening to information resources should be aware of the context of that reading/viewing/listening by relating what they find to what they already know about that topic and to the original purpose in seeking out that information resource. Secondly, there is agreement that irrespective of the type of information resources being used – print, audiovisual or electronic – there is little difference in the information skills needed by pupils to use these resources effectively and that information skills as viewed above should not be confused with technical skills such as the ability to use a videocassette player or to use Netscape to access World Wide Web Pages. Information skills, therefore, are essentially thinking skills which encourage pupils to ask themselves questions about their individual learning process. Thirdly, it can be seen that different researchers have produced similar but different lists or classifications of skills and that there are key differences in emphasis amongst some researchers, e.g. Wray and Lewis's emphasis on interaction with texts. Thus teachers and school librarians can profit from examining the work done by researchers and by using the knowledge of these researchers to good effect by examining their own curriculum and identifying which areas of the curriculum would most benefit from information skills development. Subsequent chapters will look at examples of information skills teaching in a range of schools but it is important that teachers and school librarians put these examples into the context of teaching and learning in schools before attempting to adapt these examples for use in their schools.

Information skills and IT

The availability of a range of IT based information resources, particularly in school libraries, in the form of CD-ROMs, online information services and the Internet has greatly increased the amount of potentially curriculum-related information which can be accessed by pupils at all levels of secondary education. For pupils, the use of IT based resources requires new skills in using the technology but these are low-level mechanical skills which pupils do not find difficult. Thus even first year secondary pupils will have few problems in accessing and manipulating information on CD-ROMs and their senior counterparts will not find the use of Reuters or Netscape very challenging in a technical sense. Where IT provides new challenges to pupils is in the vast amount and variety of information available in a number of different formats including text, photographic, graphic, audio and video. It is the ability of pupils to handle this huge increase in available information sources that teachers and school librarians need to examine. Otherwise, pupils may be swamped with information which they find difficult to manage and evaluate. Schools are increasingly familiar with the problems of pupils downloading sections from CD-ROMs into a word-processing package and presenting this as their own work. Thus the existence of IT based information resources provides schools with opportunities but also problems in maximizing the opportunities for pupils to use IT based resources to enhance their learning and improve the quality of their assignments. Teachers and school librarians, therefore, will seek to teach pupils to use the resources effectively by drawing their attention to the importance of recognizing both the advantages of IT based resources in the form of new and interestingly presented information but also the dangers of finding too much information, much of which may be irrelevant to their purpose.

The 'Libraries of the future' project

The NCET's 'Libraries of the future' project examined the implications of using multimedia packages, Reuters 'Business Briefing' service and the Internet in schools and identified key areas relating to information skills particularly when pupils used Reuters or the Internet to find and use information for assignments within the school curriculum. The project reported that pupils learned that planning online searches on Reuters was vital and that searches had to be planned *before* using the computer. In terms of finding information, the project reported that:

- ✔ the same retrieval skills were used with new electronic sources as with print
- ✔ planning and refining searches was even more important with electronic media
- ✔ in some projects pupils combined retrieving from both electronic and print sources of information

✔ pupils found relevant information more easily from structured information sources such as Reuters Business Briefing
✔ retrieving information from the Internet was time consuming and often difficult
✔ the type of information retrieved from the Internet was often unsuitable for curriculum use.

The NCET project also examined pupils' skills in using information retrieved and found that pupils were effectively summarizing information but that 'high levels of skills were needed to analyse and synthesise masses of information'. The ability of pupils to evaluate information found was examined and the project found evidence of pupils questioning information found in electronic sources and in some instances, the pupils checked the validity of the information in books. The project found that use of the Internet could be problematic in some areas because of the difficulty of assessing the accuracy and reliability of information and also because of the constantly changing nature of many Internet sources. In many cases, the use of electronic sources has made pupils much more aware of the need to be critical in relation to information found on CD-ROMs or the Internet.[17]

Information skills and the Internet

In the context of Canada and the USA, Johnson argues that pupils' access to the Internet has changed the nature of information retrieval in schools and he argues that, 'In the past, the researcher's major challenge was to locate enough data to make meaningful use of it. The Internet researcher has the opposite challenge: to select useful data from the glut of information on the networks of 11 million computers'.

Johnson also identifies a number of skills which pupils will need in order to make good use of the Internet and these include:

✔ knowing the difference between information and knowledge or insight
✔ sorting and evaluating information and information sources
✔ understanding the problem
✔ identifying what information is needed for a problem
✔ knowing the need to be recursive when problem solving

✔ framing essential questions
✔ identifying subsidiary questions
✔ planning a search
✔ modifying the search when new information suggests it
✔ synthesizing information to create fresh answers and insights.

Johnson acknowledges that these skills are similar to those used with print resources but stresses that these skills will be used more effectively by pupils because of the amount and variety of information on the Internet.[18]

Information skills and CD-ROMs

While the Internet may hold the key to future electronic information resources, the use of CD-ROMs in school libraries and in classrooms represents the main use of such resources at present. Atkinson and Scott argue that CD-ROMs such as those that hold full text versions of newspapers such as the *Guardian, Times* or *Daily Telegraph* are valuable resources since they 'speed up the information retrieval process, often combining searching with the ability to retrieve full text in the same process. The additional advantage to the librarian/trainer is that the interactive nature of the technology actively requires the conceptual and intellectual skills which they are seeking to develop in the student'.

The authors also state that it is important that pupils' use of CD-ROMs is preceded by search strategy formulation and that CD-ROMs are regarded as one type of information resource which pupils can use amongst a variety of sources which exist in the library.[19]

Carson refers to a project done by Key Stage 3 (12–14 years) pupils studying physics in which the pupils use IT in the classroom to examine space satellites and weather conditions and use The Physical World and Encarta CD-ROMs in the library to support their assignment work. Carson notes that print resources are also used and that, as Atkinson and Scott argued, pupils should see information resources as an interrelated totality and not as separate units of information in the classroom or in the library. Carson's approach includes providing pupils with advice on 'study skills' which includes encouragement to pupils to study the objectives of the 'Earth in Space' project and, working in groups, write down what they already know about each objective and discuss their existing knowledge. Pupils are also encouraged to monitor progress on the project and to evaluate how they have used information resources throughout the project.[20] Carson's project is a very good example of an integrated approach to the use of IT based resources in the classroom and the library as it combines guided learning through the use of worksheets and established objectives with the opportunity for pupils to use CD-ROMs to find and apply information.

Martin and Swift examined pupils' use of CD-ROMs in geography including Global Explorer and state that, when using CD-ROMs, 'Research skills are needed to help pupils select relevant sections and to make their own basic notes', but warn of pupils downloading sections from CD-ROMs and writing in 'Encarta language'. Within geography, pupils can use CD-ROMs as an information resource and Martin and Swift state that, 'What is important is the depth and enrichment that an up to date information base can give to our enquiry; the freedom and flexibility to explore, and indeed to go wrong, can enrich the research process'.[21]

Brown summarizes a range of views on the use of CD-ROMs in schools and the need for information skills in order to exploit the potential of such resources and stresses that a key skill in using CD-ROMs is the ability to reject information, stating 'we still need to be able to define what it is we want to know. Perhaps even more importantly we need to know, or be able to recognise, what we do not need . . . We do not need vast quantities of loosely relevant material; we want to be able to reach the one or two specific pieces of information that relate to our particular area of interest'.

Brown hopes that in the future, software will become more sophisticated to allow pupils to form and apply more coherent search strategies when using CD-ROMs but insists that the identification of purpose is crucial before a CD-ROM is searched.[22]

Because the use of electronic information resources such as the Internet are relatively new, it may be tempting for teachers and school librarians to overemphasize the differences between print and electronic resources and to concentrate too much on the technical aspects of these new resources. This should be resisted and pupils should be encouraged to use electronic and print sources together to satisfy a curriculum-related need for information. The skills which pupils need in order to 'read', understand and take notes from electronic resources which present ideas and information in a variety of formats also need close attention and will be referred to in later chapters.

Approaches to teaching information skills

It is universally agreed that information skills need to be taught:

✔ across the curriculum
✔ in the classroom and in the school library
✔ by the teacher and the school librarian
✔ in relation to the curricular needs of pupils at different levels of the school
✔ in relation to a range of print and electronic information resources.

In practice, however, there appears to be major stumbling blocks in schools which prevent this universal agreement from being implemented. Information skills teaching has to be seen in the context of a number of aspects relating to the structure of the school, the influence of the head-teacher, the teaching and learning styles of the school's departments, the availability of resources and the status of the school librarian. These factors tend to be different in schools across the developed countries and there is no clear pattern of practice which can be said to exist in all schools even within one district in the UK, Australia, Canada or the USA. What can be established is that successful teaching of information skills in schools depends on a positive combination of the above aspects, i.e. the structure of the school encourages cooperation between staff; the head-teacher fully supports the development of information skills across the curriculum; teaching and learning styles in the school allow for a combination of teacher centred and pupil centred education which encourages pupils to learn directly from the teacher but also independently from the use of information resources; there are adequate funds available to purchase a range of information resources which can be available to pupils in the classroom and in the school library; and the status of school librarians is such that they are seen as cross-curricular professional information specialists within the school as well as the manager of the school's library based resources.

Cooperation between teachers and school librarians

The need for cooperation between teachers and school librarians is well documented and Brown states that new teachers in particular will require an introduction to information resources in the school and that cooperation on teaching information skills should begin when the new teacher takes up post. Brown argues that an effective whole school policy will ensure cooperation on information skills teaching and that, 'This will promote common understandings, aims and objectives and assessment measures'.[23]

Johnson reinforces this message by stating that teachers and school librarians should jointly plan a series of learning objectives and lesson plans to teach pupils how to effectively use information skills in an integrated manner across the curriculum and Johnson concludes, 'It will only be through the co-operative efforts of the teacher–librarian (the research skills specialist) and the classroom teacher (the subject specialist) that this integration will occur'.[24]

Evaluation of information skills

A key aspect of approaches to teaching information skills is the extent to which there will be evaluation of the effectiveness of that teaching. Evaluation is often seen as requiring very sophisticated research skills on the part of teachers and school librarians and as something which will be very time-consuming. Selmes, however, argues that if the teaching of information skills is to be seen as an integral part of the school's curriculum, then teachers and school librarians need to evaluate how successful the teaching has been and whether any improvements or additions are needed. Selmes suggests that by using reasonably uncomplicated questionnaires, interviews with pupils and an inventory of pupil responses to a series of statements related to learning, the effectiveness of information skills teaching in the school can be gauged and appropriate action taken to rectify any problems.[25] The obvious difficulties of this approach for teachers and school librarians lie in factors such as work load and time to carry out evaluation but the rewards for both staff and pupils may be great if evaluation is successfully carried out.

Conclusion

This chapter has shown that there are a number of definitions of information skills and that a large number of discrete but interrelated skills have been identified by researchers. Few teachers or school librarians will be able to have indepth, completely up to date knowledge of new research findings in all the different fields related to information skills such as planning skills, the use of electronic resources, reading, viewing and listening skills, synthesizing skills and writing skills, but it is important that professionals in schools attempt to keep abreast of significant developments in this area (e.g. the work of Wray and Lewis) and one of the roles of the school librarian, as school information manager meeting the information needs of school staff, will be to draw to the attention of teachers new work on information skills. Teachers and school librarians can also discover the work of their professional colleagues in other schools via in-service training courses, conferences and increasingly through Internet listservs such as LM_NET[26] and World Wide Web sites. As with school pupils, school staff will be continually learning about information skills teaching and learning.

References

1 Irving, A., *Study and information skills across the curriculum*, Heinemann, 1985.
2 Marland, M. (ed.), *Information skills in the secondary curriculum*, Methuen, 1981.
3 Wray, D. and Lewis, M., 'Extending interactions with non-fiction texts: an EXIT to understanding', *Reading*, **29** (1), April 1995, 2–9.
4 Rogers, R. (ed.), *Teaching information skills*, Bowker Saur/British Library, 1994.
5 ibid.
6 Brown, J., 'Developing information skills', in Kinnell, M. (ed.), *Managing library resources in schools*, Library Association Publishing, 1994.
7 Wray, D., *Teaching information skills through project work*, Hodder and Stoughton, 1987.
8 Marland, M., op cit.
9 Tabberer, R., *Study and information skills in schools*, NFER-Nelson, 1987.

10 Wray, D. and Lewis, M., op cit.

11 ibid.

12 Eisenberg, M. and Berkovitz, R., 'The six habits of highly effective students', *School library journal*, August 1995, 22–5.
Website: http://edweb.sdsu.edu/edfirst/bigsix/basics.html

13 Brown, J., op cit.

14 Irving, A., op cit.

15 Tabberer, R., op cit.

16 Australian School Library Association, *Teaching information skills*, (CD-ROM). Forthcoming.

17 National Council for Educational Technology, *Information skills in action*, NCET, 1993.

18 Johnson, D., 'Student access to the Internet', *Emergency librarian*, 22 (3), Jan–Feb 1995, 8–12.

19 Atkinson, J. and Scott, N., 'Rethinking information skills teaching', *Learning resources journal*, 11 (2), June 1995, 45–8.

20 Carson, S. R., 'A supported self-study approach to Earth in Space at Key Stage 3', *Physics education*, 30 (2), March 1995, 95–100.

21 Martin, F. and Swift, D., 'What can CD-ROMs do for us?', *Teaching geography*, 21 (1), January 1996, 20–3.

22 Brown, J., op cit.

23 ibid.

24 Johnson, D., op cit.

25 Selmes, I., *Improving study skills*, Hodder and Stoughton, 1987.

26 LM_NET is a discussion listserv for school librarians across the world. To subscribe, email to Listserv@Listserv.syr.edu and include in the message Subscribe First Name Last name, e.g. Subscribe James Herring.

Chapter 3
Teaching

After reading this chapter, you will be able to:

✔ **understand some definitions of teaching**
✔ **outline a range of effective teaching skills**
✔ **examine methods for planning lessons**
✔ **understand how to effectively deliver a lesson**
✔ **create a positive atmosphere in a teaching context**
✔ **evaluate aspects of control and discipline in the class-room or library**
✔ **understand the benefits of team teaching between teachers and school librarians.**

Teaching information skills is, in some ways, no different from any other teaching done in the school in that those involved in the teaching require a range of skills in order to be effective teachers. There are some differences to be taken into consideration when teaching information skills and these include the nature of the skills being taught, i.e. transferable, cross-curricular skills and, in the case of teaching done in the library, the location of the teaching. As with the teaching of other skills in schools, the need for *effective* as well as *efficient* teaching is paramount and teachers and school librarians will try to maintain high standards of teaching in order to meet the expectations of pupils and to achieve curricular objectives. As the teaching of information skills will be done by a number of staff in the school, it is important that the standard of teaching should be the same irrespective of who is teaching and where they are teaching and cooperation between teachers and the school librarian can help to ensure that the standard does not vary. This chapter will provide an overview of:

✔ definitions of teaching skills
✔ the range of different skills necessary for effective teaching
✔ planning lessons
✔ delivering lessons
✔ creating a positive atmosphere in the classroom or library
✔ assessment of pupils'; work
✔ control and discipline in the classroom or library
✔ self-assessment for teachers and school librarians
✔ the need for information skills to be taught by a team of teachers and
  school librarians.

What is teaching?

Teaching has been analysed by a number of writers and researchers from many different perspectives. Teaching skills are those skills used by the teacher who seeks to achieve curricular objectives by encouraging learning amongst pupils. In order to do this, teachers need to be effective leaders, communicators and, above all, managers. Kyriacou states that, 'The essence of being an effective teacher lies in knowing what to do to foster pupils' learning and being able to do it'.[1]

Marland also emphasizes the need for effective teaching skills, stating that, 'A good teacher is a good classroom manager . . . a teacher's first task is managing the classroom'.

Marland further argues that the better prepared the teacher is, the less that teacher will have to think about managing the classroom during the lesson and that this will help the teacher to become more relaxed while teaching.[2]

Kyriacou provides an excellent overview of teaching and teachers and quotes Wragg who 'sees teaching skills as strategies that teachers use which facilitate the pupils learning something worthwhile'.[3]

This emphasis on teachers' management skills is clearly stated in the literature on teaching skills and Kyriacou provides a further example by quoting Leinhard and Green who 'argue that teaching is a complex cognitive skill based on knowledge about how to construct and conduct a lesson and knowledge about the content to be taught'.[4]

Thus teaching is not primarily related to the teacher's knowledge of specialist subjects although this is very important. In order to transfer this subject knowledge to pupils and enable pupils to learn, teachers will use a range of skills which will make them teach in a well organized and well managed manner. It is interesting to note that the language used by those defining teaching skills is based on management techniques and skills. Thus Kyriacou quotes Clark and Patterson who state that, 'For the less experienced teacher, much less of the decision making has become routine and hence there is more to think about while the lesson is in progress'.[5] As will be seen below, teaching skills emphasize aspects of management such as planning, organizing and evaluating and teachers and school librarians who teach information skills will pay close attention to teaching skills in order to provide pupils with lessons which are effectively taught, i.e. in a well managed environment in which the teacher or school librarian and pupils feel comfortable. Marland sums this up well by stating that, 'The successful teacher cares . . . teaches well . . . manages well'.[6]

Teaching skills

As with all professionals, teachers and school librarians will require a combination of different types of skills in order to be effective teachers and the most successful teachers will display an ability to seamlessly employ this range of skills and to vary their use of skills according to the needs of pupils in particular lessons. This ability to deploy skills as needed, such as changing the emphasis in a lesson from subject based skills such as map reading to more general learning skills such as note taking, come with experience. Wragg, outlining the results of the Teacher Education Project, notes that experienced teachers learn how to adapt their skills to the different needs of classes and to the reactions of pupils to particular subjects. On the other hand, less experienced teachers need to spend more time in preparing lessons in fine detail until they learn the more advanced skills of changing the emphasis or content of a lesson midway through the lesson itself.[7]

Three important areas

Kyriacou outlines a comprehensive list of teaching skills which need to be acquired. These skills include three essential areas of teaching skills which cover firstly the teacher's knowledge of his/her subject; the pupils being taught; the whole curriculum; the range of possible methods to be used;

the context of teaching and learning; the internal and external influences which exist at the time of teaching; and the teacher's own individual teaching expertise and experience. The second major factor identified by Kyriacou is decision making which is defined as 'comprising the thinking and decision making which occur before, during and after a lesson, including how best to achieve the educational outcomes intended'.

Thirdly, Kyriacou considers the actions taken by teachers during lessons and the way in which teachers behave while teaching.[8] Thus there is a need for teachers and school librarians not only to identify the range of skills required for effective teaching but also appears to appreciate that they will need to combine aspects of broad teaching strategies, for example, whether pupils will work in groups or not, with individual teaching skills such as how to use an OHP effectively in the classroom or library.

In support of the above outline, Kyriacou quotes Child as arguing that teaching skills include 'knowledge about subject matter and pupils, preparation and planning, the organisation of learning (getting the lesson started, exposition, keeping the lesson going, reinforcement and rounding the lesson off), classroom management (exercising control and discipline), the assessment of pupils' learning and the evaluation of one's own teaching'.[9] The literature on teaching skills stresses the interrelation of teaching skills to one another and that an effective teacher is someone who *combines* teaching skills rather than excels in some skills and lacks others. This aspect is perhaps one of the reasons why teaching appears to be a relatively straightforward process of presenting information and ideas to pupils and providing pupils with activities, after which learning will take place. Teaching, however, is a complex mix of skills which need to be consistently applied by the teacher or school librarian because any weakness in areas of teaching skills may affect the teacher's performance or worse, be exploited by pupils.

Kyriacou highlights the need for consistently high standards in teaching skills by examining HMI reports to identify what the *outcomes* of effective teaching should be. The key outcomes include:

> . . . lessons should be purposeful with high expectations conveyed . . . there should be the chance for pupils to organise their own work to some extent . . . the pupils should clearly perceive the lessons as relevant and should hold their interest . . . the work done by pupils should be related to their ability . . . pupils' language skills should be

developed through questioning . . . there should be variety in the lesson . . . there should be good control by the teacher of the pupils' behaviour and pupils and teachers should respect each other.[10]

Given this formidable list, which can be related to every lesson taught in school, it is clear that before teaching information skills in the classroom and the library, teachers and school librarians will be involved in much thinking, planning and organizing before the lessons take place. The integration of skills is paramount and Kyriacou argues that teaching skills are not mutually exclusive and 'all the skills involved in lesson presentation, lesson management, classroom climate and discipline are all interactive skills. In other words, exercising these skills involves monitoring, adjusting and responding to what pupils are doing'.[11]

The Four Ms

Smith and Laslett package teaching skills as 'the four Ms'. Firstly, *management* of the classroom and planning of lessons which will enhance pupils' learning which Smith and Laslett argue 'requires an ability to analyse the different elements and phases of a lesson, to select and deliver appropriate material and reduce sources of friction'.[12] The second M is *mediation*, which covers interactions with individual pupils where problems exist, helping pupils to raise their self confidence and avoiding confrontations. *Modification*, the third M, covers the planning of activities to change pupil behaviour and decisions on rewards and punishments. Finally, *monitoring* relates to checking school policies on pupil behaviour and cooperation between teachers in helping to solve problems.[13]

The following sections in this chapter seek to provide guidance for teachers and school librarians on a number of key elements in teaching but can only provide a brief overview. Reading current literature and discussion on approaches to the teaching of information skills with experienced practitioners will provide teachers and school librarians with opportunities to improve their own teaching skills and thus meet the high expectations of pupils noted above.

Planning lessons

Marland, in his excellent guide to teaching, highlights the need for the planning of lessons to be done thoroughly, with thought given to virtually all the teaching skills identified above. Marland insists that good planning not only insists that the *teacher* will be satisfied with the lesson but that the *pupils* are happier and more willing to learn when taught by a teacher who is 'organised and firm'.[14]

Poorly planned lessons, according to Marland, satisfy neither pupil nor teacher, ensure that the teacher has to work harder during the lesson and provide a recipe for potential chaos in the classroom by creating gaps in pupil activity which can lead to pupil unrest and possible teacher–pupil confrontation.

Planning information skills lessons

Teaching information skills presents teachers and school librarians with opportunities to plan well conducted, well organized lessons in which pupils learn through a variety of explanations, questioning, activities and assessment. In order to achieve these results, the planning of individual lessons as well as the sequence of lessons which may be taught covering different aspects of information skills will have to be done in some detail because of the difficulties posed in teaching information skills in schools. The difficulties include: relating the subject matter, e.g. note taking, to the abilities of the pupils; problems in teaching pupils to examine their own learning styles; the need for good organization of lessons which involve pupils working in groups in the classroom and the library; and the need for good control of pupil behaviour while teaching locational skills in lessons during which pupils will be moving about in different areas of the library.

Four main elements

Kyriacou identifies four main elements in planning lessons which include firstly deciding on the educational objectives which the lesson will aim to achieve. In teaching information skills, this could mean that after the lesson, pupils would be able to understand the concept of skimming and scanning texts. Secondly, the actual format of the lesson, which includes decisions on what activities will be used during the lesson. For example, pupils might be given an explanation of skimming and scanning, then asked to work silently on a prepared handout, then to work in groups to compare individual findings, after which the teacher or school librarian would go over the handout with the class and repeat the key points in skimming and scanning at the end of the lesson. Included in this part of the preparation for the lesson would be a script of the lesson which outlines the sequence of activities, the content of each activity and any materials which would be used. Thirdly, Kyriacou points out the need for teachers to consider 'all the props to be used including materials, worked examples, checking that apparatus is ordered, delivered and in working order, arranging the layout of the classroom and, in occasional circumstances, even a rehearsal, such as when a new experiment or demonstration is involved'.[15]

Given the increasing use of IT within the school library and the need to teach pupils aspects of information skills in relation to the use of OPACs, CD-ROMs, online databases or the Internet, teachers and school librarians using IT as part of an information skills programme will have to plan ahead in terms of checking IT equipment *before* the lesson, ensuring that connections are made or that printers are working or that downloaded examples have been gone through before being used in the lesson.

The fourth element in Kyriacou's analysis of planning lessons relates to how teachers plan to monitor and assess the progress pupils make towards achieving the educational objectives of the lesson and how the teacher might be able to assess which pupils have acquired new knowledge or skills.[16] Thus the teacher or school librarian who is introducing skimming or scanning skills to pupils will have to decide in advance which methods are to be used to evaluate pupils' progress in understanding the concept of skimming and scanning and in applying the skills. This might take the form of an exercise completed by pupils or by questions to groups of pupils. Whichever method is to be used, planning the form of this evaluation, how long it will take and how it will fit into the overall lesson plan, need to be decided in advance.

The rhythm of teaching

Marland discusses planning in the context of what he calls 'the rhythm of teaching' and states that, 'A lesson has to be organised as a sequence arranged in time . . . The pupil is stimulated by a good use of time and bored and irritated by a bad use'.[17]

Pupils are sophisticated consumers of the services offered by teachers and school librarians and are constantly evaluating teachers' performances in relation to their own learning and to opportunities for exploiting a teacher's lack of planning and classroom management. Marland emphasizes the need for teachers to be aware of the importance of timing involved in breaking a lesson up into individual parts and the need to concentrate on what pupils will be *doing* and not merely what they are learning. Planning should also stimulate teachers to vary the activities within lessons and the format of lessons, so that the pupils are not fed on an unchanging diet of exposition, activities and conclusion.[18]

Delivering lessons

No two teachers will deliver a lesson in exactly the same way as delivery will be affected by a number of factors including the location of the teaching, the personality of the teacher, the relationship which exists between the teacher and the pupils and the pupils' interest or otherwise in what is being taught. Despite this, there are generally agreed criteria about what constitutes the effective delivery of a lesson and how teachers can improve the delivery of lessons by paying attention to some fundamental rules of good teaching.

A number of authors emphasize the need for a positive start to the lesson and its impact on the subsequent progress of the lesson. Smith and Laslett add four rules of teaching to the four Ms seen above. Rule 1 is 'get them in' and covers the need for teachers to welcome pupils and state clearly what is to be done once the pupils are seated.[19] Marland also stresses the need for a planned start to the lesson and suggests that every pupil should have something to do once they enter the classroom, whether this be reading part of a textbook or reading a handout. The use of the blackboard to provide instructions will help to maintain a smooth start. Teachers can avoid problems with late arrivals by ensuring that pupils are occupied as soon as they enter the classroom.[20]

The purpose of the lesson

The need for pupils to understand the purpose of a lesson and the expectations which the teacher has about what pupils are expected to achieve may seem very obvious but Marland writes that some teachers do not give pupils sufficient explanation at the start of the lesson. Marland argues that not only do pupils have the right to know what the lesson is likely to contain but that they will feel more confident about the lesson once they have been told of its content. Marland urges teachers to inform pupils in clear language what the lesson is about, how it will be organized, what pupils will learn and what activities pupils will be involved in. Marland backs up this argument by stating that, 'For too many pupils, most lessons are a more or less exciting mystery tour, in which they never know how long they are going to be at one activity before they are set down and whipped off for another'.[21]

Bell and Solity agree with Marland's approach, stating that pupils need to know why they are to complete certain tasks, whether they will have choices during the lesson, what they as pupils will gain from the lesson and also what the teachers expect from the pupils in terms of accuracy, speed of work and use of language. Pupils also need to know at the start of the lesson whether they are to work individually or in groups, where they are to work and whether there are restrictions on movement during the lesson.[22]

These factors are important to pupils but can often be underestimated by teachers who may be tempted to launch into lessons without preparing the ground first. In this author's experience, a lack of suitable explanation at the beginning of a lesson unsettles pupils who may be tempted to ask awkward questions to the teacher during the lesson, indicating that, despite the fact that half of the lesson has elapsed, they are not certain about the purpose of the lesson. This can lead to the teacher having to spend time in the middle of the lesson giving an explanation which should have come at the start. For many pupils, this can lead to more confusion and often unrest amongst the pupils. For teachers and school librarians teaching information skills , the explanation given at the start of the lesson will be vital because of the need for pupils to understand the importance of how they as individuals learn and the need for them to learn skills which will help them learn more effectively. Without clear explanations of the purpose of lessons for example, note taking, pupils will easily lose interest in what they might see as abstract exercises.

Pupils' activities

Once the purpose of the lesson has been laid out, pupils should then be asked to complete an activity or should be introduced to a topic. In this explanation or exposition part of the lesson, teachers and school librarians will plan what is to be explained, how long the explanation will take and how the explanation will be presented. Given the pupils' likely attention span and the need to maintain their interest, explanations of concepts such as note taking should be reasonably short and immediately followed by an activity such as reading a handout or completing a work sheet. Kyriacou states that the middle section of a lesson should stimulate pupils' interest in the topic via good use of resources and related activities for individuals or groups to complete.[23]

Marland notes that while worksheets are useful and popular, teachers should avoid giving pupils 'an interminable diet of worksheets'. If worksheets are used, Marland states that pupils should be given a clear explanation of what the worksheet is for and how long pupils have to complete the worksheet. Marland also argues that while posing questions to the class or individuals is a useful technique, it must done in such a way that pupils learn from the questions. Questions should not be too difficult and teachers should use answers to further explain concepts. Asking questions is a difficult skill to acquire, in Marland's opinion, but by emphasizing the positive use of questions to stimulate pupils into thinking about different aspects of a topic, teachers will become more adept at asking questions.[24] In teaching information skills, teachers and school librarians can usefully follow Marland's advice by posing questions which enable pupils to think about their own information skills. For example, a school librarian might ask pupils to consider how identifying key words will help in planning a project and gather in positive responses to use as further explanation.

Finishing off the lesson

Lessons also need to finish off well if learning objectives are to be achieved and if pupils are to feel a sense of achievement. Smith and Laslett's Rule 2 is 'get them out' and they argue that a good lesson can be spoiled by a poor ending. Pupils should be given early warning of the end of the lesson, perhaps five minutes before they are due to leave. Once pupils have finished work and/or returned materials and *are ready to listen*, the teacher can go over what has been achieved in the lesson and look forward to the next lesson. Smith and Laslett argue that good endings to lessons provide 'an opportunity to refresh, restate and reinforce the theme of the lesson'.[25]

Once the summing up has been completed, pupils will be able to leave the classroom or the library in an orderly fashion. Teachers and school librarians will be careful to avoid trying to conclude the summing up with the actual end of the lesson as pupils will not be effective listeners if they are on their way out of the classroom or library.

Creating atmosphere

The atmosphere in which pupils work can add a great deal to their motivation in the classroom or library if positive steps are taken by the teacher or school librarian to create a climate in which both staff and pupils can relax and in which there is an air of mutual respect. A number of factors contribute to creating a positive atmosphere and Wheldall and Glynn argue that what they term as 'antecedents' such as heating, lighting, the arrangement of seating and generally welcoming surroundings, contribute to a pleasant atmosphere.[26] Marland echoes this by stating that the classroom's 'arrangement, displays, atmosphere and practical details will contribute to the class management, the learning, the relationships and the pleasure of working together collaboratively'.[27]

Kyriacou uses adjectives such as purposeful, task oriented, relaxed, warm and supportive to outline the importance of creating a suitable climate for learning. Added to this, Kyriacou argues, are the ways in which teachers motivate pupils. Teachers need to take into account both intrinsic motivation, i.e. the natural curiosity of pupils who seek to discover things for themselves, as well as extrinsic motivation, i.e. the desire of pupils to seek praise from the teachers or to gain qualifications. Teachers should have high but realistic expectations of pupils, Kyriacou notes, as pupils will respond to a positive climate created by the teacher.[28]

The key to creating a positive, relaxed atmosphere in the classroom or school library will lie with the performance of the teacher or the school librarian. Marland's insights into the importance of how well the teacher can communicate with pupils are shrewdly expressed. Marland argues that, 'For a significant part of his or her professional life, every teacher is a performer, using voice, facial expression and gesture'. The atmosphere of the location of the teaching, whether it be in the classroom or school library, will be significantly affected by the confidence shown by the teacher when speaking to pupils. Marland advises teachers to take careful note of important factors to be recognized when addressing pupils. For example, pupils must be *ready* to listen, they must all be in the class, be seated, able to hear and silent, before the teacher talks to them. Marland's advice on speaking to the whole class is 'choose your moment; decide what you're going to say; use a suitable manner'.

Speaking to pupils

The teacher's voice is also a crucial element in teaching and Marland advocates an approach to speaking which will demonstrate the teacher's interest in what is being said as this will, in turn, generate interest in pupils. Marland advises that, 'Your voice must be clear and you must have a sense of speaking to the group . . . the key is intensity not volume'. A teacher speaking to a group of pupils can also heighten interest by looking at different parts of the class and at different individuals because, as Marland states, 'This way you can establish an intimacy with the pupils that always assists order and enriches communication'.[29]

Using humour

Experienced teachers and school librarians acknowledge that using humour can also help to create a positive atmosphere but that humour must be used sensitively and in a way which does not cause embarrassment or offence to individual pupils. Humour should not be used as a method of criticizing the individual pupil's behaviour, lifestyle or beliefs and thus teachers and school librarians will not be telling jokes to pupils in the same way that pupils tell jokes to each other. However, humour can be useful in helping pupils to feel relaxed in the classroom and Marland notes that teachers can share a joke with pupils to good effect, especially if it is at the teacher's expense. In this way, the teacher can be seen as someone who does not view teaching as a cold, intense practice. Marland advises teachers not to take their tasks too seriously as 'humourless indignation and sad intensity alienates their charges'.[30]

The atmosphere of the classroom or school library is, therefore, a subtle combination of a number of environmental and human factors and it is the teacher or school librarian who can ensure that pupils feel able to contribute to this atmosphere by respecting their surroundings and acknowledging the efforts made on their behalf. Inexperienced teachers and school librarians will need time to adjust to the different atmospheres which sometimes exist with different groups of pupils or in different locations but pupils will expect whoever is teaching them to be consistent in their approach to creating a good climate. Given the stresses of working in a school, teachers and school librarians will find it difficult often to maintain this consistency of approach but if pupils feel that they know what to expect of the teacher and if they recognize that the teacher *does* show interest in the pupils as well as in the subject, pupils are more likely to respond positively and contribute to a relaxed but learning-oriented atmosphere in the classroom or in the school library.

Pupil behaviour

A further aspect affecting the creation of a good atmosphere in the classroom or school library relates to the establishment of an understanding amongst pupils and teachers as to what constitutes acceptable behaviour. This is a complex issue as different types of behaviour will be acceptable or not acceptable depending on the activities taking place. Thus in some instances, for example when the teacher or school librarian is talking to the pupils as a group, it will be unacceptable for pupils to talk to each other. In other instances, for example when pupils are in the library and using CD-ROMs, pupil discussion may be positively encouraged. The key aspects of pupil behaviour are the teacher's or school librarian's knowledge of the complexity of pupil behaviour; the establishment of agreed rules; methods of discipline and consistency of approach.

The behavioural model

A number of authors outline the contribution of the behavioural model in helping teachers to understand the issues relating to pupil behaviour. Bell and Solity state that the behavioural model takes the view that 'behaviour is learned and that what we learn and the ways in which we behave depend on our everyday experience and the environment in which we live.' The behavioural model therefore puts stress on what can be observed, on what pupils actually do and not on individual interpretations of pupil behaviour. Bell and Solity argue that teachers should concentrate on pupils' behaviour in terms of agreed positive outcomes rather than on potential misbehaviour and that the behavioural approach 'provides a framework for consistent management which stresses the importance of helping children to show appropriate behaviours from the outset, rather than waiting for them to happen'.[31]

Establishing rules

The behavioural model also outlines the importance of establishing rules within the learning situation and there is general agreement in the literature that these rules should be discussed with pupils and agreed norms established which both pupils and teachers should respect. Bell and Solity state that rules can cover interactions between pupils or between pupils and teachers; work done in school, for example the need to listen; and specific rules such as those relating to the handing in of assignments. Bell and Solity argue that effective rules should be 'clearly worded; phrased positively, brief and to the point and few in number'.

Rules can be drawn up by teachers and explained to pupils, with examples of positive and negative aspects being outlined. Bell and Solity's view is that teachers and pupils should have joint ownership of rules but that if this is to happen pupils need to be able to discuss the rules and make suggestions as to amendments. Rules should be clearly displayed in the classroom and teachers should be encouraged to display the rules, to draw pupils' attention to them on a regular basis and to praise pupils' good behaviour when the rules are followed, i.e. rules should not be only referred to when they are contravened.[32]

Wheldall and Glynn also state that, for rules to be effective, they must be agreed by both pupils and teachers and they provide an example of rules displayed in a home economics class:

✔ We try to work quietly and put our hands up when we need help
✔ We listen carefully to instructions and read the board and our recipe sheets carefully
✔ We try to work tidily in our units and share the jobs when cleaning away
✔ We get on with our cooking without disturbing others.

Having rules displayed in this way allows the teacher to remind pupils of the contract into which they have entered with the teacher. An effective teacher will be able to point to the existence of the displayed rules without having to repeat any or all of the rules in order to create a positive approach amongst pupils.[33]

Discipline

Discipline covers a range of actions taken by teachers and school librarians to correct unwanted behaviour which may cause disruption within the learning environment. Pupils can be well disciplined without being oppressed and effective discipline will come from the existence of rules, the attitude of the pupils and the attitude of the teacher. Thus discipline can be seen as both positive and negative. If a class is working effectively and has a good relationship with the teacher or school librarian, then that class can be observed as demonstrating good discipline. Discipline in schools is too often regarded as existing only in the negative sense in that pupils are only disciplined when they misbehave. Marland argues that the teacher who shows effective class management will have fewer problems than the ill prepared teacher as lack of planning can create opportunities for misbehaviour. Marland argues that all teachers need to criticize pupil behaviour from time to time but 'generally speaking, when you need to criticise, do it clearly and briefly, do not dwell on it and, above all, avoid a tirade of abuse directed at an individual'.[34] Kyriacou concurs with Marland's analysis, stating that teachers should 'make good use of general teaching skills and pre-emptive strategies to minimise pupil misbehaviour occurring'.

Kyriacou argues that private reprimands for pupils are more effective than public criticism and also that behaviour should be criticized, not the pupil. In correcting misbehaviour, teachers should invite positive actions from pupils, by, for example, asking them to get their work done in the time allowed rather than stating the negative and obvious, i.e. that there is too much noise.[35]

Bell and Solity's extensive analysis of what they term 'constructive discipline' examines the factors which affect unwanted behaviour in the classroom and they point out that the physical setting such as how the classroom is laid out, the educational setting such as the appropriateness of tasks and the social setting such as whether individual pupils are aware of rules, all affect pupils' behaviour. Bell and Solity also argue that how pupils view the consequences of their behaviour will be important in determining how they behave. This does not merely refer to possible negative consequences such as the teacher criticizing the behaviour or the withdrawal of privileges but relates to how the pupils view the teacher's behaviour. Thus if a teacher regularly raises his or her voice, pupils may do the same but if there is an atmosphere in which normal conversations can occur between teachers and pupils, then pupils are more likely to identify the positive consequences.[36]

Avoiding confrontations

The need to avoid confrontations with individual pupils is paramount in teaching and teachers and school librarians faced with potentially hostile pupils need to appreciate the importance of learning how to cope with possible confrontations. Confrontations can occur when the response of an individual pupil to criticism of his/her behaviour is taken as a personal attack. There may be many reasons for pupils behaving in this way and some of these reasons may well lie outside the school. Kyriacou states that, in dealing with confrontations, teachers should 'stay calm . . . defuse the situation . . . be aware of the heat of the moment . . . design a mutual face saver . . . use social skills . . . get help if necessary'.[37]

There will be policies in the school on how teachers and school librarians should deal with pupil misbehaviour and these should be followed exactly. Inexperienced teachers and school librarians should be aware of what steps to take if they feel threatened by a pupil and this may involve asking a more senior colleague to come in and defuse the situation. Confrontations will be rare events in most lessons and it is important that teachers and school librarians recognize that they themselves should not cause confrontations, for example, by making threats which they cannot carry out and that individual pupils may have personal problems, in which case guidance teachers should be consulted.

The behaviour of pupils in the classroom and school library will thus be influenced by a number of factors as seen above and the creation of mutual respect between the pupil and the person teaching that pupil will contribute greatly to the avoidance of problems with pupil behaviour.

Assessment of pupils' work

One aspect of teaching information skills will be that teachers and school librarians will present pupils with a number of formative or summative assessments in order to establish whether pupils have understood the concepts and skills which they are taught. Kyriacou outlines the key aspects of assessment and argues that assessment 'involves a whole range of skills regarding selection, design, implementation, match of activity to purpose, marking procedures, feedback and appropriate and valid use of the results of assessment'. When pupils are given assessments, they need to have a clear understanding of the purpose of the assessment, the expectations of the teacher and how pupils can meet these expectations. Assessments also need to be closely matched to the activities undertaken by pupils. If pupils are unclear about why they are doing assessments or what the criteria for success will be for a particular assignment, they are unlikely to be motivated in completing the assignment. Pupils also need to be given good feedback on assignments, in Kyriacou's opinion, and feedback should be 'sufficiently speedy, thorough, constructive and helpful, so as to foster and sustain pupils' motivation and self confidence and facilitate further progress'.[38]

Kyriacou refers to the work of Weston who argued that assessments produced negative outcomes if: there was too much emphasis on norm referenced assessments which weaker pupils would find difficult and would inevitably gain low marks; there were too many summative assessments; assessments were too narrowly cognitive and academic; the pupils were 'passive receivers of assessment practices with little say in the process involved or awareness of the criteria being used'; and if there was too much emphasis on the aggregation of marks which could hide good results for some pupils. Weston further argued that assessments should be more individually targeted and that pupils should be aware of the aims of the assessment and where possible, involved in its design.[39]

Assessments given to pupils when they are being taught information skills will vary according to which aspect of information skills is being assessed. Assessing pupils' knowledge and skills in this area can be difficult in that teachers and school librarians will attempt to teach information skills not as a separate subject but as part of the skills needed by pupils to successfully complete assessments in the subject which they study in school. Thus, in most cases, assessments should be based around work done by pupils within a subject area. For example, if pupils are being assessed in terms of how they understand the need to carefully plan assignments in history, then the assessment of their knowledge and skills in this area should be closely related to the activities they are doing with the history teacher. Otherwise, there is a danger that pupils will not appreciate the need for the assessment or may see it as an abstract, discrete exercise which does not relate to their other work in school.

Team teaching

Teaching information skills across the curriculum will involve a number of teachers as well as the school librarian in the development of a coherent curriculum which introduces and reinforces concepts and skills in information skills. When the skills are being taught, in order to ensure that pupils view information skills as core learning skills which are transferable across subjects, there will necessarily be a need for cooperation between teachers and the school librarian. Team teaching, to be effective, should present pupils with a curriculum which contains lessons taught in some instances, by a teacher or a school librarian and in other instances by both a teacher and the school librarian.

Firstly, the teaching team should have a good understanding of what each person in the team is teaching so that there can be cross references made in individual lessons to other lessons. For example, the school librarian may remind pupils of the importance of using key words in locating information and refer back to a lesson on planning assignments done by a teacher. Secondly, the pupils should not have the impression that each member of the team is teaching a different course. Thus at the beginning and end of each lesson, there should either be recapping of what was previously done or a look forward to what pupils will be learning in the next lesson. Thirdly, it is useful for the team to adopt a house style when preparing handouts or worksheets for pupils, so that the pupils feel that all the lessons can be grouped together as a recognizable course. Lastly, team teaching will involve teachers and the school librarian in extra work in terms of planning meetings to develop and review the teaching but team teaching can add value to lessons in information skills in that pupils can benefit from the shared knowledge and expertise of different professionals in the school.

Conclusion

What is clear from this review of teaching skills is that teachers and school librarians will recognize that teaching is complex and the performance of the person who is teaching and the response from pupils depends on the wide variety of factors noted above, including the teaching environment, the attitude of both teacher and pupils; the use of relevant resources and the extent to which the teacher or school librarian is able to manage. What Marland calls 'the craft of the classroom' will be improved only by experience and self-assessment and Marland notes perceptively that, 'The craft won't work without the spirit compounded of the salesman, the music hall performer, the parent, the clown, the intellectual, the lover and the organiser but the spirit won't win through on its own. Method matters'.[40]

References

1 Kyriacou, C., *Essential teaching skills*, Blackwell, 1991.
2 Marland, M., *The craft of the classroom*, 2nd edn, Heinemann, 1993.
3 Kyriacou, C., op cit.
4 ibid.
5 ibid.
6 Marland, M., op cit.
7 Wragg, E., *Classroom teaching skills*, Routledge, 1984.
8 Kyriacou, C., op cit.
9 ibid.
10 ibid.
11 ibid.
12 Smith, C. and Laslett, R., *Effective classroom management*, 2nd edn, Routledge, 1993.
13 ibid.
14 Marland, M., op cit.
15 Kyriacou, C., op cit.
16 ibid.
17 Marland, M., op cit.
18 ibid.
19 Smith, C. and Laslett, R., op cit.
20 Marland, M., op cit.
21 ibid.

22 Bell, S. and Solity, J., *Classroom management: principles and practice*, Croom Helm, 1989.
23 Kyriacou, C., op cit.
24 Marland, M., op cit.
25 Smith, C. and Laslett, R., op cit.
26 Wheldall, K. and Glynn, T., *Effective classroom learning*, Blackwell, 1989.
27 Marland, M., op cit.
28 Kyriacou, C., op cit.
29 Marland, M., op cit.
30 ibid.
31 Bell, S. and Solity, J., op cit.
32 ibid.
33 Wheldall, K. and Glynn, T., op cit.
34 Marland, M., op cit.
35 Kyriacou, C., op cit.
36 Bell, S. and Solity, J., op cit.
37 Kyriacou, C., op cit.
38 ibid.
39 ibid.
40 Marland, M., op cit.

Chapter 4

Whole school policies on information skills

After reading this chapter, you will be able to:

✔ **identify the key factors in developing whole school policies on information skills**
✔ **evaluate the experiences of teachers and school librarians in two case studies**
✔ **understand the need for communication and cooperation between professional staff in schools.**

One element which can be identified in schools which have successfully implemented information skills programmes across the curriculum is the existence of an agreed policy towards the teaching of information skills. In some schools, policies are formal and written in detail whilst in other schools, policies are less formal and take the form of broad aims and objectives relating to learning outcomes. The need for active cooperation across departments and for support from senior management is clear in these schools. The development of whole school policies and programmes is examined in this chapter by a review of existing research and by two case studies carried out as part of a research project at The Robert Gordon University by Mike McConnell and Dorothy A. Williams.

Whole school policies on information skills

As the need for information skills in all areas of the curriculum is recognized more and more in schools, the need for schools to have a clear policy on what skills are required, where they are to be taught in the curriculum, how they are to be taught, when they are to be taught (and reinforced), how the policy will be evaluated and reviewed and who will be responsible for coordinating a whole school policy on information skills, is also being examined. In the barrage of new initiatives and policies imposed on schools from outside the school, it is often difficult for teachers and school librarians to take the necessary steps back to examine objectively the teaching of information skills in a particular school. This is often mainly due to constraints of time rather than a lack of willingness to pursue this issue. Some key factors have been identified as being prerequisites for the development of a whole school policy on information skills and these include the need for support from senior staff, a review of skills within curricular areas, identification of overlap between curricular areas, an examination of teachers' and school librarians' knowledge of learning skills, the development of a written policy on information skills across the curriculum and a programme of in-service training on information skills within the school.

The role of senior management

Selmes argues that 'With the support of the headteacher, a group of committed teachers within a school could initiate activity and develop materials with subject departments'. Selmes sees support of senior management as being crucial but also states that committed teachers can also, by example, demonstrate to others how developing study skills (Selmes's term) can improve the pupils' approach to learning. He argues that a whole school policy can be developed 'alongside inservice sessions concerning the process of learning and the importance of the teachers' influence on this process'. The constraints identified by Selmes include lack of time for teachers, staff resources and other curriculum developments within the school.[1]

Rogers states that the establishment of a whole school policy should be coordinated by 'an experienced member of staff who knows the issues, can develop materials and working strategies, and is able to support other teachers'.

Other factors recognized by Rogers include:

✔ the headteacher's positive attitude
✔ staff sharing curricular and organizational responsibilities

✔ the commitment of staff to work in their own time to develop methods and materials, and

✔ to assess their relevance to other areas of the curriculum.

Rogers also recognizes the need to maintain commitment to such a policy by staff and states that this can be done by demonstrating the value of such a policy across the curriculum and by continued in-service training within the school.[2]

Brown states that before producing a whole school policy 'staff must have a common understanding of what is meant by information skills and an audit of what is currently happening needs to be undertaken so that staff development and resourcing needs can be assessed'. Brown also argues that it is important for teachers and school librarians to recognize that there may be subject specific information skills such as measuring and evaluating experimental results within science, but it is important that subject based teachers recognize that there is a great deal of overlap within learning skills. Inservice sessions can help to bring together subject departmental views on information skills and provide the basis for a whole school policy.[3]

Experience in further education

Morrison and Markless examined information skills development in further education but many of their findings could equally apply to schools. They identified a number of problems with the teaching of information skills in further education colleges which included a view of information skills as being:

✔ fragmented in pockets of diversity
✔ frequently small in scale
✔ often lacking in focus and not made explicit
✔ initiated and implemented at various levels in the college hierarchy
✔ characterized by different degrees of cooperation between library and teaching staff.

Morrison and Markless stress the commitment of senior college management as being vital and insist that a strategic view of information skills is necessary and they argue that information skills development needs to be part of the overall planning in colleges. Morrison and Markless argue that this can be done by: 'Preparing a clear statement of aims and objectives for the college, including a statement about the type of learning to be provided for students; seeking shared understanding of the implications of developing skills; and conducting a curriculum audit in which information skills are included'.

Staff development for teaching staff and librarians is also seen as vital as are in-service sessions on information skills across the curriculum and the importance of viewing the library as a varied and changing collection of learning resources.[4]

Links to other initiatives

As was stated above, schools are faced with a large number of new initiatives with which they have to cope in a limited timescale and the development of information skills may be seen as competing with other curricular initiatives. However, teachers and school librarians can usefully link information skills to other developments especially in areas such as reading, differentiation or information technology, in order to convince senior school management that a whole school policy on information skills does not represent a wholly separate approach to teaching and learning in the school but can, and should, be allied to other developments.

Case study 1: Webster's High School, Kirriemuir

Webster's High School is a rural secondary school with a roll of 700 pupils. An information skills policy is being developed out of an existing study skills programme for S1 and S2 (first two years of secondary school). The information skills programme within the Year 1 geography syllabus (see later chapters for examples) is seen as an exemplar in the school and similar programmes are being adopted by other departments.

Origins of the policy

The origin of the information skills policy lies in a working party set up in 1994 to address the issue of information skills within all years of the school. The working party concentrated on Years 1 and 2 and the existing library skills programme was expanded and taught by six departments to give a cross-curricular approach. Audiovisual aids and study skills books were purchased for use with Years 4–6 and an information skills resource bank was developed within the teacher resource section of the library. Using geography as a basis, a list of information skills which could be taught by all departments was drawn up. The working group then audited existing skills within the school for six months and produced an 'Information skills pilot' which attempted to relate both research theory and existing practice within the school as a coherent whole. Specifically, it related the skills audited to Marland's model. The pilot sought to prove that the geography course had noticeably improved information skills in pupils and concluded that it had. It is clear that this pilot was far from prescriptive and that the emphasis was on encouraging teachers to use information skills by the good example of other departments.

Key factors

The successful introduction of information skills to the syllabus at Webster's High School was brought about by a number of factors, some of which reflect the research cited above. Firstly, the head teacher (and consequently senior management) was extremely supportive of the initiative and of the librarian and placed great emphasis on the library as a central and integral part of all teaching. Secondly, it appeared that the school librarian had unofficially assumed the role of the coordinator of the programme and she had exceptionally good knowledge of information skills research. She was the focus of good communication in the school and her position was consolidated by the strong support she received from senior management. Thirdly, the school was not over-reaching itself as the information skills programme was based on existing knowledge within the school and tried to build on this. Although advancement was incremental and gradual, the progress that has occurred so far has been strong, practical and has gained wide support because the information skills policy was not seen as a 'bolt on' extra within the school.

There were other factors which were idiosyncratic to this school and which contributed to the success of the policy. The enthusiasm and personality of the key individuals involved was vital as was the knowledge and experience of the school librarian, her status and the availability of a large and well equipped library. These factors will be different in each school but must not be underestimated when considering the potential success of an information skills programme in a school.

The school librarian's view

The school librarian argued strongly that any information skills programme in the school had to be clearly integrated into the curriculum if it was to succeed. The programme also had to be part of a whole school policy relating to the library and the availability of IT resources in the library and in the classrooms. She stated that communication with staff especially in the dissemination of research had led to a more flexible and open approach to information skills within the school. The school librarian's knowledge of educational initiatives such as the Scottish 5–14 and Higher Still initiatives was also important as she could not expect teachers to be interested in library initiatives unless she was aware of educational initiatives. The school librarian stated that in-service training for teachers in the school was a vital part of the early stages of information skills development as it allows teachers to keep up to date with developments and ensures that new teachers are inducted as soon as possible into the school's information skills ethos. The development of a teachers' resource collection in the library provided a good back up to in-service training. In terms of promoting information skills policies and programmes in the school, the school librarian believed that senior management, principal teachers, teachers from feeder primaries and herself should be involved in a working group to audit information skills across the curriculum and a policy should be developed to fit the needs of that particular school. She argued that, in Webster's High School, teachers were often wary of new cross-curricular initiatives which were seen as being imposed from outside the school but the gradual development of the information skills policy, involving a 'bottom up' approach combined with support from senior management, had proved to be an effective way of introducing a cross-curricular programme. The school librarian hoped to see more in-service training for both teachers and school librarians in the future on cross-curricular initiatives; better current awareness services for schools and more opportunities for school librarians to work with secondary and primary teachers on the 5–14 initiative which covered developments for pupils aged 5–14 in both primary and secondary schools in Scotland.

The geography teacher's view

The geography teacher argued that two key factors dominated the initial development of information skills programmes in the school. The first factor was time, in which to develop the curriculum, attend the working group, to get agreement with teachers in other departments, work with the school librarian and evaluate the effectiveness of the programmes. The second key issue was terminology in that there had to be agreement across the school on what was meant by information skills and how this term differed from, for example, study skills or research skills. The Country Profile project became the focus of the geography teacher's interest in information skills. He decided to develop an earlier investigative project into an in-depth inquiry which involved the pupils identifying key words, designing a suitable search strategy, employing a range of library based and IT based skills and choosing a presentation format. This approach allowed marking to be broken down into constituent parts which allowed pupils to isolate the areas in which they were weakest, rather than merely presenting them with an overall mark. The project also included a self-assessment section at the end where pupils could comment on their own performance (see Chapter 10). The geography teacher viewed the school library as a central part of the school and an indispensable feature of an effective information skills programme. Communication and cooperation with the school librarian, with senior management and with other teachers were essential elements for information skills planning, according to the geography teacher. He valued the contribution of other teachers in reinforcing the skills which the pupils used in their geography project as this increased the probability of transferability across the curriculum. Like the school librarian, the geography teacher saw information skills developments as being *part* of new initiatives such as Higher Still and 5–14, and not as a separate initiative.

The headteacher's view

In the headteacher's opinion, the development of information skills at Webster's High School had been successful because it had been based on cooperation between a cross-section of staff in the school and had not been based on one person's ideas. He argued strongly that having a policy on information skills was not sufficient in itself but what was vital was creating the communication necessary to establish a whole school policy based on awareness of need and coherence in terms of definition. The headteacher viewed the audit of where information skills were already being taught (consciously or unconsciously) in the curriculum as a very important step in policy formation and he viewed the incremental approach as being necessary if the policy was to be effective. The headteacher praised the enthusiasm of those involved in the initiative, particularly the geography teacher and the school librarian, and stated that this enthusiasm had spread to other teachers who could now see the need for information skills across the curriculum and the benefits to be gained. He argued that initiating such a policy was not without problems particularly of time and of the definition of information skills but his view was that, once staff had been convinced of the value of an information skills policy, there was a basis for such a policy being prescriptive.

Case study 2: Grantown Grammar School

Grantown Grammar School is a small rural secondary school with a roll of 350 pupils. It has a comprehensive information skills programme in place which includes structured modules for years 1–3, the adoption of a SCOTVEC module for teaching information skills to years 5 and 6 and project work in all years which integrates information skills with work of departments. This has been achieved despite the school being in a less well funded region, with a small library budget and a school librarian who is responsible for this school and another school in the region. This contrasts with Webster's High School which is relatively well funded and has a full time school librarian. Both schools, however, are similar in that they have very enthusiastic and knowledgeable school librarians, strong support from senior management and teachers who see information skills as core to the curriculum.

The origins of the policy

In this school, the school librarian had tried to introduce a programme of information skills based on experience in a previous school but had done this in isolation from the curriculum. This was recognized as an interim step by all concerned and discussions between teaching staff and the school librarian led to agreement over what the programme should include. Problems of definition arose because of the teachers' previous experience with terminology such as research skills, library skills and resource based learning. This was resolved through agreement that a prescriptive terminology was not necessarily needed if there was a common core of skills recognized and taught across the curriculum. The integrated project undertaken by first year pupils (see Chapter 8) encouraged cross-curricular teaching of information skills and led to economies in preparation time for teachers and the school librarian. As with Webster's High School, the information skills policy had emerged from pilot programmes run by one or two departments which was followed by a general adoption of information skills as core skills across the school. The approach, therefore, was incremental until all departments had recognized the need to teach and reinforce information skills.

Key factors

The success of the information skills programme in this school, despite limited financial resources, is undoubtedly due to the cooperation between staff and a receptive attitude to new ideas. The piloting of programmes in the early stages in a small number of departments served as examples to other departments and the programme had developed incrementally. A further feature was strong support from the school's senior management who recognized the need for information skills to be taught across the curriculum and gave active support to the development of a policy. The knowledge and enthusiasm of the school librarian and the teachers involved in the early stages of the programme were vital components.

The science teacher's view

This teacher's interest in information skills initially arose from educational research which he was undertaking and he saw clear links between a number of areas of educational research and research on information skills. In this teacher's view, the ease of communication in a small school had greatly helped the informal discussions on information skills teaching which had followed the arrival of the new school librarian. Initial problems with terminology and the need to base information skills in the curriculum had been overcome through joint discussions facilitated by the open attitude of the staff and the support of the depute rector. The school librarian's (unofficial) role as research coordinator in the school had also aided the development of the information skills programme. The strength of the school's programme lay in its organic nature, in that there was a significant amount of autonomy afforded to departments within agreed overall learning outcomes. In science, elements of the information skills programme could be modified to suit particular learning outcomes but reinforcement across science subjects was standard.

The school librarian's view

The school librarian admitted that her attempt to adapt an information skills programme from a previous school was problematic because of the need to develop a programme to each school's particular needs. She argued strongly that the receptive attitude of teachers to information skills had been a key factor in the development of a whole school policy and that mutual professional recognition between school librarians and teachers was a prerequisite for success in this area. The school librarian had initially worked with the English department although she recognized the dangers of possible lack of transferability of skills in this approach but once the science department agreed to participate, others followed. The school librarian's status at Grantown was fully recognized and this led to recognition of her role as research coordinator and information skills facilitator. She identified problems in terms of the time needed for in-service work and the lack of cover for the school librarian and the need for the school to have a full time school librarian. The school librarian's view was that the incremental approach taken by herself and other teachers had led to a well developed, well tested and integrated programme in the school.

The depute headteacher's view

From a management point of view, the depute head teacher argued that as well as achieving educational objectives within the school, the information skills programme had been designed to produce economies of time in relation to the avoidance of duplication of preparation across different departments. He agreed that it was not possible to impose a programme on the school and the programme's success had been based on strong staff interest and enthusiastic cooperation between teachers and the school librarian. He argued that the information skills programme needed to be spread to the feeder primary school so that pupils were not faced with a completely new approach when they arrived at secondary school. The depute headteacher recognized the need for more in-service training in the school and that financial problems did affect the school's curriculum. However, he argued that information skills were not so integrated into the curriculum that budget limitations would not restrict the programme. More money for IT and library developments was needed in the school but a limited budget necessarily restricted these developments.

Conclusions

The two schools cited above clearly echo some of the key factors in information skills developments seen in recent research. The case studies do show, however, that application of research findings in a school is not always easy given the peculiarities of different schools and the personnel involved. The incremental approach taken by the schools above shows that a gradual emergence of a whole school policy rather than an imposed policy was a key factor in the success of the programmes. Thus the key factors which can be identified from these case studies are:

✔ a clear definition of information skills tailored to the school's requirements
✔ a comprehensive audit of existing skills and needs
✔ support for developments from senior management in the school
✔ convincing teachers of the validity of information skills by good example
✔ status of and support for the school librarian
✔ communication, aided by working groups and in-service training
✔ integration of information skills within the curriculum
✔ a clearly defined role for the school librarian as research coordinator and facilitator of the information skills programme.

The need for whole school information skills programmes and policies are recognized but each individual school will have to examine local factors in order to decide how to approach the development of such programmes. From the research review and from the case studies, it is clear that active professional recognition and cooperation between teachers and school librarians and strong support from senior management are vital factors in the success of any information skills programme.

References

1   Selmes, I., *Improving study skills*, Hodder and Stoughton, 1987.
2   Rogers, R. (ed.), *Teaching information skills*, Bowker Saur/British Library, 1994.
3   Brown, J., 'Developing information skills', in Kinnell, M. (ed.), *Managing library resources in schools*, Library Association Publishing, 1994.
4   Morrison, M. and Markless, S., *Enhancing information skills in further education*, British Library, 1992.

Chapter 5
Purpose

After reading this chapter, you will be able to:

✔ **examine the importance of pupils' existing knowledge in relation to purpose**
✔ **evaluate methods of brainstorming for pupils**
✔ **understand the use of key words in the information skills process**
✔ **examine methods of concept mapping**
✔ **evaluate methods of identifying information resources in the classroom, the school library and outside school.**

The effectiveness of how pupils identify the purpose of the assignment or project which they are asked to complete by the teacher is a major issue in information skills teaching and learning in secondary schools. If pupils do not clearly identify the purpose of their work then they will not be able to plan their work well; they will not know what kinds of information they need nor what the appropriate sources of information and ideas might be; they will be unclear about how to use sources such as what to read and what to take notes on; and they are unlikely to present a well written, logically designed and structured assignment. Teachers' comments on pupils' work very often relate to the issues of how pupils have covered the topic in question, i.e. whether they have chosen too wide a topic which they cannot cover or too narrow a topic on which there is too little information available. On the other hand, pupils are often not specifically taught how to identify the purpose of their work and it is often assumed that pupils will either know how to do this instinctively in secondary school or they will have learned how to do this in primary school. In many cases, neither is true. In many schools now, much more attention is paid to encouraging pupils to *think* about their assignment work in some depth before progressing on to the further stages of finding and using information sources in the library or in the classroom. Thus identifying purpose is a cognitive skill which pupils may have practised to some extent in primary school but teachers and school librarians in secondary schools need to identify what experience the pupils actually have in practising thinking skills before assuming that pupils will use these skills.

This chapter will examine a number of aspects related to purpose and cover aspects of the pupils' existing knowledge, brainstorming and identifying questions, identifying key words, concept mapping and identifying information resources. In this and subsequent chapters, reference will be made to the existing literature and examples of good practice from schools will be included.

Pupils' existing knowledge

Wray and Lewis argue that pupils need to examine their existing knowledge of a topic before they can acquire new knowledge on that topic and they stress that teachers need to make sure that pupils themselves realize that this is a key step in establishing purpose. Wray and Lewis encouraged teachers in their project to use brainstorming and concept mapping in order to bring the pupils' attention to their existing knowledge since if the pupils acquire new knowledge but do not relate it to existing knowledge, they are likely to forget it fairly quickly.[1] Carson's approach is in a context where pupils are given set objectives within a physics assignment, e.g. 'understand how gravity affects how satellites (including the moon and the earth and the planets round the sun) travel'.

In the guidance given to the pupils, under the heading of 'study skills', Carson's pupils are told: 'Before you begin, you should (as a group of 3 or 4) try to write a sentence or paragraph on each of the objectives. This will help you find out how much you know about each one, and so which ones you need to concentrate on'.[2]

The importance of the pupils' existing knowledge is often underestimated and in many information skills programmes seen by this author, there does not appear to be enough stress on asking pupils to define their existing knowledge before they begin to explore a new topic. A key element in *purpose*, therefore, should include in pupils' guidelines the question, 'What do I already know about this topic?' and pupils can then be asked to write down not only what they know but how they gained this knowledge. Assignments will emerge from the existing curriculum and senior pupils undertaking an assignment on the causes of World War 1 will be able to identify:

- ✔ what they have learned from the teacher
- ✔ what they have learned from reading/listening/viewing in the class-room
- ✔ what they have learned from other sources, e.g. reading/viewing in the library.

This would provide pupils with a discrete knowledge base from which to approach their new assignment.

Brainstorming and identifying questions

Tabberer saw the need for teachers to allow pupils the opportunity to explore the purposes of their assignments without too much direction and the project asked questions such as, 'Do pupils get the opportunity, alone or in groups, to pour out their own ideas, to brainstorm, to think both divergently and convergently, to think round a problem, to view it later-ally, or to play with a problem by inverting the issue, posing similar or contrasting situations in order to illuminate it?'.[3] Wray and Lewis argue that pupils need to 'specify as precisely as possible what they want to find out and what they will do with that information when they have found it' and that pupils should be encouraged to write down what questions they need to ask and what tasks they need to complete in order to answer the questions.[4] Eisenberg and Berkovitz, under the heading of 'task defini-tion' state that, 'Using a school assignment as an example, students need to know the questions that need to be answered, and what kind of infor-mation is needed to answer these questions'.[5]

McKenzie and Davis stress that teachers should ask pupils to discuss a new topic in groups and state that pupils will tend to follow the style of the teacher when posing questions. Thus if the teacher suggests informa-tion type questions such as, 'List the six main causes of the Civil War' then pupils will respond with similar questions. If the teacher poses more divergent questions such as, 'Why did Lincoln only free slaves in the rebel states?' then pupils will respond with equally divergent questions.

McKenzie and Davis identify four rules of brainstorming where:

1 all contributions are accepted without judgement
2 the goal is a large number of ideas or questions
3 building on other people's ideas is encouraged
4 far out, unusual ideas are encouraged.[6]

Examples from schools

The following examples demonstrate how some schools approach the processes of brainstorming and identifying questions. In all of the examples, teachers and school librarians have worked together, in different subject areas, to produce material which provides guidance to pupils at the start of their assignment process.

At Mary Linwood School, the Library Resource Centre Action Plan (see Figure 5.1) is designed to fit into the pupils' personal organizers which cover all curricular areas and the Step by Step Guide, in this case related to work in English (see Figure 5.2), is used as a standard framework for information retrieval across the school, although it should be noted that 'information retrieval' in this context encompasses the full range of information skills which pupils use when completing assignments.

Lothian Region's School Library Service working party of secondary school librarians produced 'Information skills for seniors' and Figure 5.3 combines aspects of both establishing pupils' existing knowledge and brainstorming.

The information and study skills units produced by Preston Lodge High School, Ross High School and Musselburgh Grammar School's 'Effective Teaching and Learning Strategies' group provides a good example of how pupils can be given a general exercise on brainstorming (see Figure 5.4) and a more specific guide to identifying questions through brainstorming (see Figure 5.5)

LIBRARY RESOURCE CENTRE ACTION PLAN.

NAME: FORM:

SUBJECT:

Research Title:

Please answer these questions as fully as possible in consultation with your teacher before you leave the classroom

What do I want to find out?

*Which resources do I think will help me? (e.g. information books, encyclopae-
dia, atlas, Information finder CD ROM, resource pack etc.)?*

*Likely Library headings: e.g. Religion, Geography, Technology, Sport. (See
Subject Guide in Personal Organiser).*

*Do I want a lot of information or just
a little?*

*Am I going to read, take notes,
browse for ideas, print out information ...?*

*Do I need to work on my own or
with a partner/group?*

Time required?

Teacher's signature: .... Date: ....

Additional suggestions from Librarian:

Fig. 5.1 *Library Resource Centre Action Plan from Mary Linwood School*

Year 7. English / LRC: INFORMATION RETRIEVAL

A STEP BY STEP GUIDE TO HELP YOU RESEARCH YOUR CHOSEN TOPIC.

You will be researching your topic in the Library Resources Centre. You should
look for information in the NON-FICTION books, including ENCYCLOPAEDIAS,
and from CD-ROMS. You are going to present the information you find in a
booklet. Follow these steps:

> STEP 1 - PLANNING

What is your topic? _____

What do you want to find out about this topic? BRAINSTORM your topic to show
all the words you can think of which are related to it:

> Topic:

Fig. 5.2 *Guidance on information retrieval from Mary Linwood School*

PLANNING YOUR RESEARCH

Before you start a piece of research you must **plan** what you are going to do. That means deciding what has to be done – which resources might be useful, where to find them, and how best to use the sources of information.

Ask yourself the following questions:

1   **What do I need to do?**

     What do I already know about the topic?

     What do I have to find out?

     What is the aim of my research?

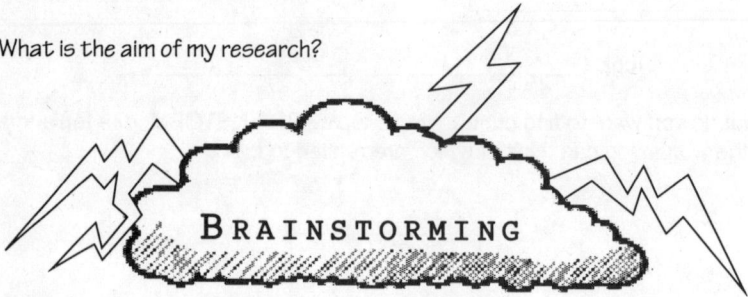

BRAINSTORMING

Make a note of all the words you can think of connected with the topic

Fig. 5.3 *Brainstorming guidance for senior pupils from Lothian Region School Library Service*

Source: *Information skills: how to help seniors survive*, School Library Service, Lothian Regional Council, 1996. (Reproduced by permission of Lothian Regional Council)

Study the diagram below carefully. You will see how one question leads to another until we are finally able to work out a basic **plan**.

Only after we have finished planning do we start doing.

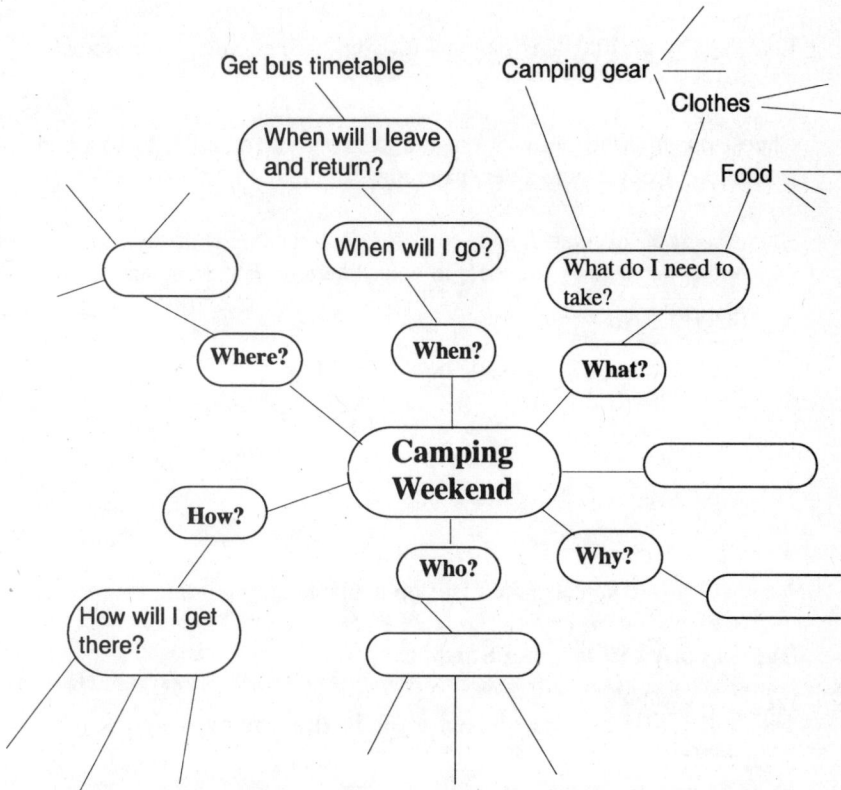

Get bus timetable

When will I leave and return?

When will I go?

Camping gear

Clothes

Food

What do I need to take?

When?

When?

Where?

What?

Camping Weekend

How?

Who?

Why?

How will I get there?

Jotting down questions, answers and ideas in this way is called

BRAINSTORMING!

Information Skills - Section 2 - Page 2

Fig. 5.4 *Brainstorming example for pupils of Ross High, Preston Lodge and Musselburgh Grammar schools*

Pupils' Notes - Section 2 - Topic 2

PLANNING

Topic 2 - Asking Questions

Look back at the diagram you drew for your brainstorming exercise on "Scotland".

Choose one branch from your diagram which you would like to do a mini project on. Copy it onto a new page in your jotter.

Choose part of this branch and see if you can come up with any further ideas which may be useful. Add them to your diagram. For example:-

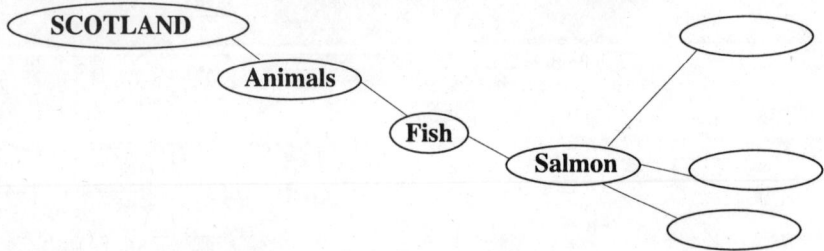

You have now completed the first step in planning - choosing your topic!

Take a copy of Planning Sheet 1.

Fill in the title of your chosen topic in the box provided for "Topic Title".

Now we are going to use our key question words to help us fill in a planning sheet for our mini project.

Remember the key question words -

What? Who? Why? When? How? Where?

Information Skills - Section 2 - Page 5

Fig. 5.5 *Identifying questions at Ross High, Preston Lodge and Musselburgh Grammar Schools*

Key words

In order for pupils to effectively use their brainstorming sessions, many schools focus on the need for pupils to identify key words in relation to their chosen topic. This process allows pupils to think through their topic in terms of its parameters, e.g. if pupils are doing an assignment covering the role of the UK parliament, will they cover the origins of parliament (a historical viewpoint), what is decided by parliament (a regulatory viewpoint) or the role of MPs within parliament (a functional viewpoint)? By asking pupils to identify key words, teachers and school librarians are helping pupils in a number of ways. Firstly, the identification of key words in a new topic establishes a firm link with the pupils' existing knowledge. Secondly, if pupils are encouraged to identify key words using the terminology learned in the classroom, they are more likely to be able to use the key words when seeking information. Thirdly, key words can be used when pupils are searching for information such as in the library's OPAC (Online Public Access Catalogue) or in books or in CD-ROMs. Fourthly, key words can be used to provide pupils with a structure to their assignment when pupils are taking notes or writing up their assignment. The work of Williams and Herring although done in the mid-1980s is still relevant today and is used in a large number of schools in relation to enhancing thinking skills amongst pupils preparing assignment strategies in the classroom. Figure 5.6 shows how central the role of key words can be in the information skills process which can be seen as an information flow between pupils, resources and teachers. This diagram does not pretend to highlight *all* the key skills such as reading skills or synthesizing skills, but does indicate the process which pupils and teachers follow. It also indicates that if pupils *fail* to identify key words effectively at the planning stage, then it will be very difficult for them to find, select, reject and organize the information and ideas they need to complete their assignment. Thus pupils may well have to retrace some of the steps in the process if, for example, they find that the key words they identify either produce too much information (the key words are too broad) or too little information (the key words are too narrow) when searching the library's OPAC.[7]

4 (b) THINKING ABOUT FINDING AND USING INFORMATION

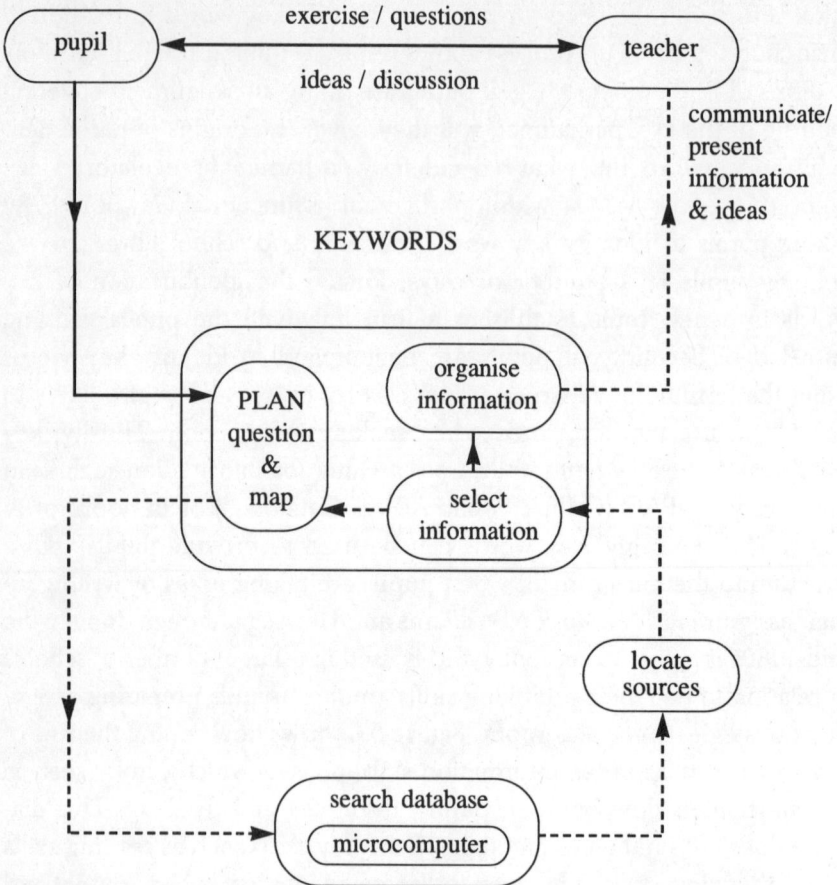

Fig. 5.6 *The importance of key words from* Keywords and Learning

For school librarians, the importance of key words to the information skills process highlights the need for school library automated catalogues to be a mirror image of the school's curriculum in that when pupils are searching for key words using curriculum based terminology, they should find that the OPAC uses the same terminology in relation to the library's books, journals and other sources. Teachers and school librarians also need to be aware that when pupils use CD-ROMs to search for material using their key words, there may be differences in the use of terminology where the CD-ROMs use language based on USA curricula.

The following examples link in with those shown above in relation to brainstorming and identifying questions in that one result of such brainstorming sessions will be the identification of key words. Figure 5.7 shows how Lothian Region's group follow up the brainstorming section with a section on key words.

—————————————————————————— Information Skills for Seniors

PLANNING YOUR RESEARCH

Before you start a piece of research you must **plan** what you are going to do. That means deciding what has to be done – which resources might be useful, where to find them, and how best to use the sources of information.

Ask yourself the following questions:

1   **What do I need to do?**

What do I already know about the topic?

What do I have to find out?

What is the aim of my research?

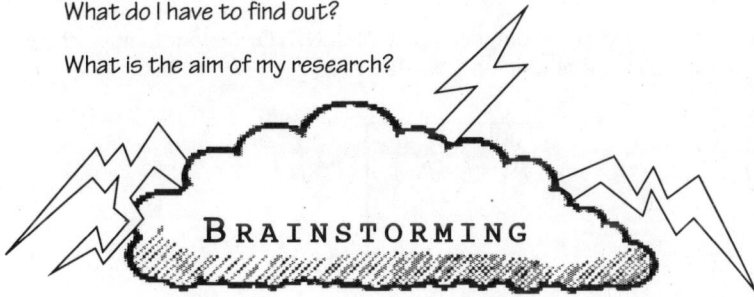

BRAINSTORMING

Make a note of all the words you can think of connected with the topic

Now make a list of **key words** which you might use to search for information.

Fig. 5.7 *Identifying key words – guidance from Lothian Region School Library Service*

Source: *Information skills: how to help seniors survive*, School Library Service, Lothian Regional Council, 1996. (Reproduced by permission of Lothian Regional Council)

Figure 5.8 shows a similar example from the Mary Linwood School and Figure 5.9 shows how the Country Profile assignment done by geography pupils at Webster's High School links key words to brainstorming.

Year 7.　English / LRC:　　INFORMATION RETRIEVAL

A STEP BY STEP GUIDE TO HELP YOU RESEARCH YOUR CHOSEN TOPIC

You will be researching your topic in the Library Resources Centre. You should look for information in the NON-FICTION books, including ENCYCLOPAEDIAS, and from CD-ROMS. You are going to present the information you find in a booklet. Follow these steps:

STEP 1 - PLANNING

What is your topic? _____

What do you want to find out about this topic? BRAINSTORM your topic to show all the words you can think of which are related to it:

Topic:

Now choose 4 of these aspects of your　　　＿＿＿＿＿＿　　＿＿＿＿＿＿
topic which you would most like to
research:　　　　　　　　　　　　　　　　＿＿＿＿＿＿　　＿＿＿＿＿＿

These are now your KEYWORDS.

Fig. 5.8 *Identifying key words – guidance from Mary Linwood School*

Country Profile

Task: Choose a country which you would like to
study.
Draw a map of the country.
Find out TEN geographical facts about the
country.

Name of country

Give two reasons for choosing this country:

1. _____

_____

2. _____

_____

Choose TEN **key words** from the classroom **brainstorming**
exercise.
Key words will help you in your search for country profile
information.
Remember to include PHYSICAL and HUMAN features.

Key Words

1. **Location**   2. _____
3. _____   4. _____
5. _____   6. _____
7. _____   8. _____
9. _____   10. _____

Fig. 5.9 *Selecting key words in Webster's High School's 'Country Profile'
project*

Concept mapping

Whitaker argues that psychological research has shown that not all learners think in a linear and sequential fashion and that many use different
facets such as word association and visual memory when thinking about
ideas and concepts. Whitaker refers to Buzan's well known 'mind maps'
which asks pupils to place their topic at the centre of the page and make
maps by identifying the key aspects of their topic. Whitaker also states
that pupils can often profit from using visual memory and should be
encouraged, where appropriate, to include visual images and colour as

well as text, when creating concept maps. Such maps, Whitaker explains, helps pupils 'to create their own classification as a means of extending the mind in its struggle for insight and understanding'.[8]

Claxton states that pupils need to be able to 'detect and build up structure in the material being studied' and that the use of concept maps will enable pupils to take a holistic view of their topic and identify problem areas within their topic such as what they do *not* know about some aspects of their topic. If pupils fail to do this, Claxton argues, they will not be able to ask the right questions and may give up easily. Using concept maps helps pupils to explore their topic and pupils can learn from group discussions of topics where concept maps are constructed in groups.[9]

Examples from schools

Figure 5.10 shows an example from 'Keywords and learning' of a key word map done by pupils and Figure 5.11 provides guidance to pupils of Ross High, Preston Lodge and Musselburgh Grammar schools on using spider diagrams. Pupils can be encouraged to discover what kind of concept map or plan suits their own individual learning style. In some cases, pupils may prefer to list their ideas as opposed to using a diagrammatic form such as spider or tree diagrams. The form of the concept map is not as important as the process of thinking about the topic and asking questions about the topic which produces a map or list of key words or phrases identified by the pupil.

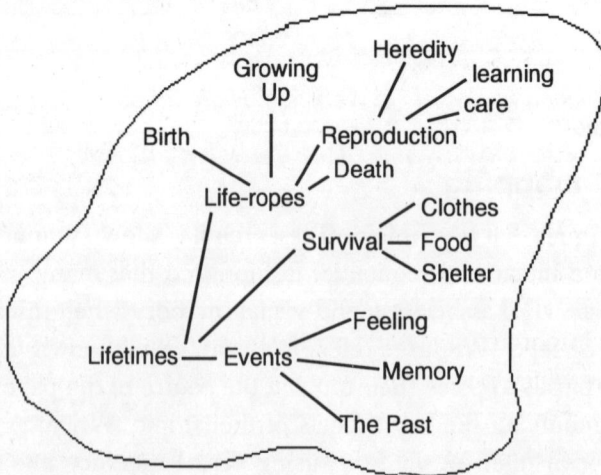

Fig. 5.10 *Example of a key word map from* Keywords and Learning

Ways of Recording and Presenting Information

1. Spider Diagrams

Spider diagrams take a key word as a heading. The heading is then broken down into various sub-classes.

For example, if we are looking at **colours** as our key word, then colours can be broken down into two main sub-classes – primary colours and secondary colours. We can then list the various colours for each sub-class.

We show this in the form of a diagram like this:

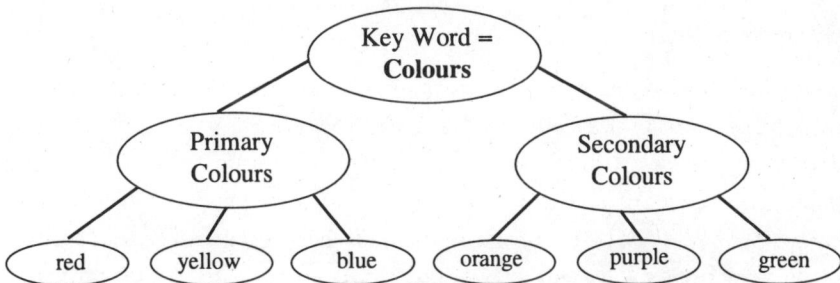

With a spider diagram we can see at a glance how things fit into an overall pattern.

Fig. 5.11 Example of a spider diagram from Ross High, Preston Lodge and Musselburgh Grammar schools

Identifying information resources

The *identification* of information resources should not be confused with the actual location of these resources in the library or in the classroom. Pupils doing assignment work can be encouraged to follow through their thinking about the topic, their existing knowledge of the topic, the iden- tification of key words using a concept map by further thinking about which information resources they might use to complete their assign- ment. It is important that this step in the information skills process is not seen as one which pupils complete when they reach the library. If pupils are expected to use the library's resources effectively, then they should have thought about the range of resources they might use *before* they reach the library. In many cases, when pupils are asked to consider what information sources they might use, they limit their thoughts to the school library whereas, if encouraged to think and discuss sources amongst themselves, they will come up with resources such as people, e.g. teachers, parents, librarians, or resources in the classroom as well as in the school library. Figure 5.12 shows an example from Hinchingbrooke School's Nine-Step Plan which stresses the importance of asking questions about information resources. Figure 5.13 from Webster's High School is a good example of encouraging pupils to think about sources in diverse locations both within and outside the school. Figure 5.14 shows St Machar Academy's Learning Plan as a whole and within the 'research' element, pupils are encouraged to identify information resources.

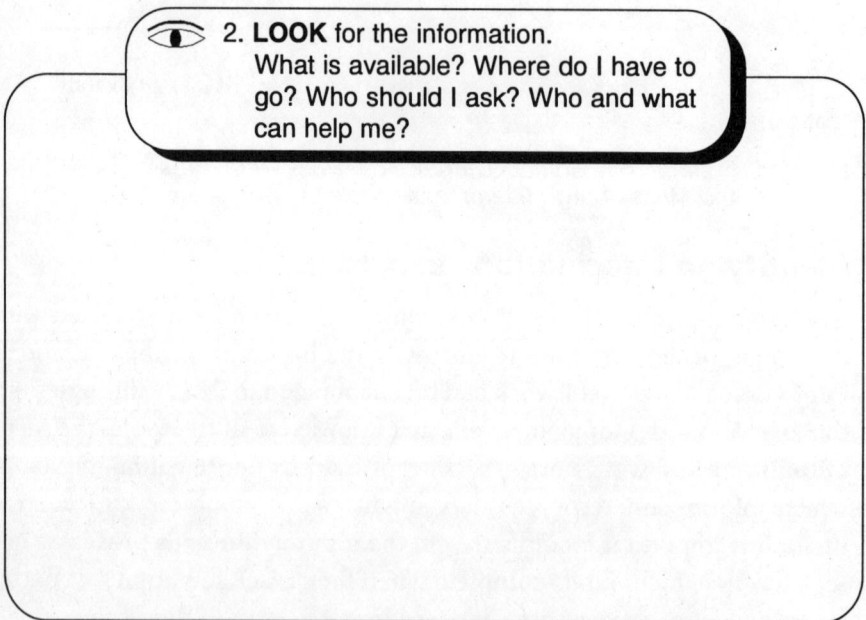

2. **LOOK** for the information.
What is available? Where do I have to go? Who should I ask? Who and what can help me?

Fig. 5.12 *Looking for information at Hinchingbrooke School*

Country Profile

(**Locating**)

You are now ready to carry out your research.
You must find out the answers to your **Key questions** listed on page 2.

You need to use a range of sources.

What kind of sources are there?

(CD Rom)   (   )   (Encyclopedia)

(   )   **Sources**   (   )

(Information books)   (Population data Sheet)   (Tourist Brochures)

Add any other sources in the empty boxes.

Write **L** beside the sources located in the Library.

Write **C** beside the sources located in the classroom.

Using **EASL** – Computerised catalogue system in the school library.

EASL can be used to find out if the Library has any books about your chosen country.

Follow the steps on the chart on the next page.

Fig. 5.13 *Identifying sources in Webster's High School's 'Country Profile' project*

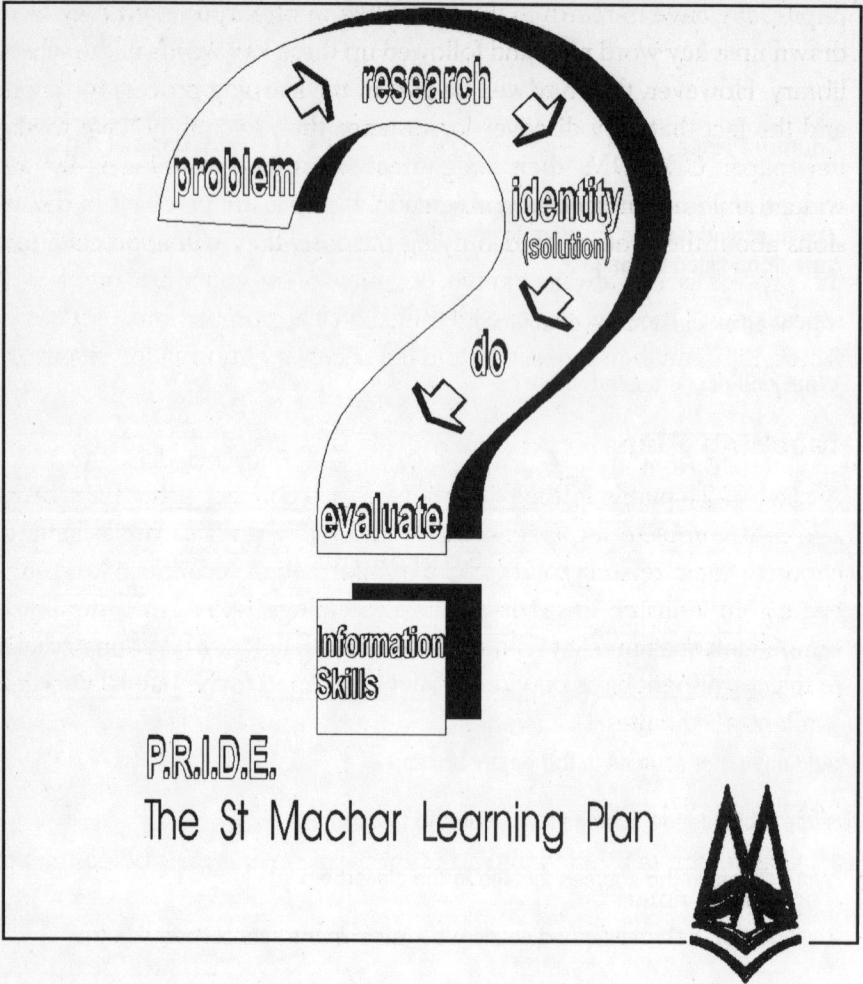

Fig. 5.14 *Researching information sources at St Machar Academy*

Conclusion

If pupils can identify the purpose of their assignment or research problem i.e. why they need information and ideas, then they will have established a firm foundation for their coursework as all other stages in the process lead on from this identification of purpose and all subsequent steps in the process relate back to this key step. It will, of course, not always be possible for pupils to fully appreciate the scope of their assignment, i.e. what the parameters of purpose are, without doing some initial reading and pupils may have to return to the identification of purpose *after* they have drawn up a key word map and followed up these key words in the school library. However, this may well be part of the learning process for pupils and the fact that they discover for instance that, once they have used a newspaper CD-ROM, their assignment on urban planning is far too wide, should not be seen as problematic. If pupils are involved in discussions about the process of identifying purpose, they will appreciate that the process is not always simple but may often contain a number of repeat steps. Once pupils have identified a clear purpose and a set of key words, they can then proceed to find the necessary information resources.

Teaching Plan

A class of 24 pupils in their fourth year of secondary school are being asked to complete an assignment in computer studies. Pupils have to choose a topic relating to an aspect of information technology and society, e.g. in industry, in services such as banking, in local or central government, in the home, at school. The format, length and marking criteria of the assignment have previously been explained to the pupils. Each lesson lasts 40 minutes.

Lesson 1: Purpose

1 Class enter, get settled and an assignment sheet is distributed to each pupil (5 minutes).
2 The teacher briefly explains that the aims of the lesson are to:

   ✔ introduce pupils to the PLUS model
   ✔ examine why purpose is so important
   ✔ examine the consequences of not clearly identifying purpose, i.e. more work for pupils and lower marks for the assignment
   ✔ allow pupils to discuss their purpose with others (5 minutes).

3 Pupils, having already had one week to think about their topic, are asked to write down the purpose of their assignment under the heading, 'What is my assignment about?' and are asked to draw a concept map of their topic. Pupils do this individually and are then asked to

work in groups of four to compare purposes and to agree on an answer to the question 'Why is purpose so important?' (20 minutes).

4 A selection of pupils are asked to give examples of purpose and to read out the answer to the question posed. Pupils' responses are praised and/or suggestions are made for improvements (5 minutes).

5 The importance of purpose is restated and pupils are asked to think about the next stage of their assignment – identifying information resources – by next week. Assignment sheets are collected in and the pupils leave (5 minutes).

References

1 Wray, D. and Lewis, M., 'Extending interactions with non-fiction texts: an EXIT to understanding', *Reading,* 29 (1), April 1995, 2–9.

2 Carson, R., 'A supported self-study approach to Earth in Space at Key Stage 3', *Physics education,* 30 (2), March 1995, 95–100.

3 Tabberer, R., *Study and information skills in schools,* NFER–Nelson, 1987.

4 Wray, D. and Lewis, M., op cit.

5 Eisenberg, M. and Berkovitz, R., *Information problem solving: the Big Six skills to library and information skills instruction,* Ablex, 1990.
    Website: http://www.edweb.sdsu.edu.edfirst/bigsix/basics.html

6 Mackenzie, J. and Davis, H., *Filling the toolbox: classroom strategies to engender student questioning.*
    Website: http://www.pacificrim.net/~mckenzie/toolbox.html#
    Beginning

7 Williams, D. A. and Herring, J. E., *Keywords and learning,* RGIT, 1986.

8 Whitaker, D., *Managing to learn,* Cassell, 1995.

9 Claxton, G., *Teaching to learn,* Cassell, 1990.

Chapter 6
Location

After reading this chapter, you will be able to :

✔ **evaluate pupils' use of the school library to locate relevant information resources**
✔ **understand the links between identifying purpose and using information resources**
✔ **appreciate the problems pupils may face in using CD-ROMs and the Internet**
✔ **prepare a lesson on an aspect of pupils' use of the school library.**

In order for pupils to successfully complete coursework of different kinds, they will be required to find and use a range of different information resources, often in different formats. In the author's non-systematic review of practice in schools in the UK in particular and elsewhere in the developed world, it often appears that too much emphasis is still given to the pupils' ability to find information and in particular, to find information in libraries. However, as this book demonstrates, there are significant moves away from this approach in many schools. This does not mean that pupils do *not* need to acquire skills in locating information but it implies that finding information should be seen as:

✔ part of the overall information skills process but not as the beginning of that process
✔ related inextricably to identification of purpose, use and self-evaluation within the information skills process
✔ as a fairly small part of the sequence of teaching information skills
✔ as being based within curricular topics when the skills of finding information are introduced or reinforced.

It should also be noted that the mechanical skills of finding information whether in a book or on a CD-ROM, for example on gravity within a physics assignment, should not be seen as the same as the cognitive skills of selecting, understanding and synthesizing information, ideas and concepts relating to gravity which are found in the book or CD-ROM. It is this underestimation of cognitive skills and overestimation of mechanical skills which has, in some cases, led to justifiable criticisms of the non-curriculum related approach taken to information skills by some school librarians.

This chapter will examine location skills in relation to the use of libraries and library catalogues, the use of books and journals, the use of CD-ROMs, the use of the Internet and the use of people as information resources. Examples from schools will be included to provide examples of good practice.

Using libraries

In the National Curriculum Orders for Key Stages 3 and 4, there are several references to the use of libraries. Within English, the Orders state that, 'Pupils should be introduced to a wide range of non-fiction texts, e.g. autobiographies, journals, diaries, letters, travel writing, leaflets' in the classroom and in the library.

Within the school library, pupils are expected to: 'use their knowledge of the alphabet to locate and find information (Level 3); locate and use ideas and information (Level 4); and retrieve and collate information from a wide range of sources (Level 5)'.

Within Information Technology, pupils should: 'explore information held on IT systems, showing awareness that information exists in a variety of forms (Level 1); and use IT to access stored information, following straightforward lines of enquiry'.

In Modern Foreign Languages, pupils should: 'use dictionaries and reference materials; use books or glossaries to find out the meanings of new words; and [read] authentic materials such as information leaflets, newspaper extracts, letters or databases'.[1]

Brown cites the results of an in-service course organized by NCET in which teachers and school librarians identified the following skills in relation to locating information in a library:

✔ use the library subject index
✔ use the library catalogue
✔ locate items on the library shelves and in filing cabinets
✔ understand the concepts of a controlled vocabulary of key words
✔ locate resources on a database
✔ plan and make visits
✔ understand the browsing principle
✔ understand that appropriate sources must be consulted if the required information is to be found.[2]

Introducing the school librarian

When pupils make their first visit to the school library at the beginning of their first year in secondary school, it is important that they gain a positive impression of the library but particularly of the school librarian. Most pupils will only have met a professional librarian in the public library and may only have met a library assistant. Thus expectations of the school librarian are likely to be low. School librarians should outline their role in the school as well as in the library and should use terminology suitable for a Year 1 class. Thus a detailed explanation of how school librarians are responsible for the management and development of the school's print and electronic learning resources is not likely either to be understood by pupils or to hold their attention. It is better to introduce school librarians as being the same as teachers in that they are there to help pupils learn and enjoy school but also as being slightly more than a teacher in that they can provide pupils with individual help in using books and other resources which will help them with their project work. Pupils from primary/elementary schools will be very familiar with project work but probably not familiar with a reasonably large library with an OPAC and CD-ROM stations. School librarians can also, in a *short* introduction tell pupils what school activities they are involved in outside the library, e.g. drama productions, sporting activities, school trips, IT clubs, etc. In an INSET course for school librarians run by the author, it was suggested that pupils could be posed a short series of questions (no more than five minutes) which focused on how they perceived the school librarian and what experience they themselves had of using libraries.

Introducing pupils to the library

While pupils need to be given an introduction to the library and how to use it effectively, they do *not* need an extensive course on what the library is and how to use it. In the past, this author has seen some well-meaning but educationally Neanderthal examples from school libraries in the UK and the USA of *five-week* courses for first year pupils in which pupils spent five 40-minute sessions learning about alphabetical order, the Dewey Decimal System, the parts of a book, the author catalogue, the subject catalogue, etc. This intense focus on the library, often in a context completely divorced from the actual curriculum, appears to have died out in today's schools but, as was noted above, there does still seem to be too much focus on the mechanics of the library and not its intellectual content.

Introducing pupils to the library can be seen as part of an introduction to information resources in the school in general. Figure 6.1 shows the induction programme outline from Easthampstead Park School and the programme is taught via geography, history, English and IT lessons.

Most school librarians produce leaflets outlining what is in the library and leaflets such as that shown in Figure 6.2 from Cramlington Community High School provide the pupils with necessary information about the library. The leaflet is given to pupils when they watch a short video about the library and Cramlington Community High School have developed a multimedia guide to the library. The guide was designed by the school librarian and teachers and developed by senior pupils.

AIMS OF THE INDUCTION PROGRAMME

1 To introduce pupils to the library in a such a positive way that they feel confident and at ease in their use of the library.
2 To reassure all pupils that libraries and books are for them, whatever their age and ability.
3 To teach pupils how to use library resources and to encourage effective use of available resources.
4 To teach, encourage and reinforce information retrieval skills.
5 To encourage pupils to work quietly and creatively in a studious atmosphere.
6 To emphasise the importance of the library across the curriculum.
7 To demonstrate to all pupils the inestimable enjoyment of the written word

---

Fig. 6.1 *Easthampstead Park School's induction programme*

CRAMLINGTON COMMUNITY
HIGH SCHOOL

LEARNING RESOURCES CENTRE

WHAT'S IN IT

FOR YOU?...

OPENING TIMES

MON-FRI	8.45 am	-	4 pm
TUES/WED	8.45 am	-	4 pm
	5.30	-	8.30 pm

Your teacher may also let you use the LRC for research and group work during lessons.

HELP DESK

Here you can book computers, television and video, cassette players, slide projectors..... buy things like pens, paper and files.... borrow, return and renew books and tapes ..... request and reserve books. Ask the Librarian and the LRC assistants for any information you need.....

WHAT YOU CAN BORROW

Y9-11 2 items for 2 weeks

Y12-13 6 items for 2 weeks

Tickets are kept in the LRC. Simply bring your books to the Help Desk to be issued. Books must be returned to this desk before the date stamped on the label.

Cassettes may be borrowed for 2 weeks for only £1. Get a 50p refund on each tape returned on time!

To borrow an item someone else has out simply ask the Librarian to reserve it for you. If we do not have the item you need we can borrow it from another library.

REMEMBER

A security system will sound an alarm if you forget to have items officially issued at the desk!

You are responsible for items on your tickets. Late return, loss or damage must be paid for!!

WHAT YOU CAN USE

COMPUTERS

... linked to the school network for word/ processing, desktop publishing, databases, spreadsheets, multimedia program creation and more! Very popular at break and lunchtime - must be booked in advance.

CD-ROM

... a large (and ever increasing) range of titles for every subject from cinema to science, art, music, encyclopedias - even rugby.

REFERENCE COLLECTION

...If you've got the questions we've got the answers on everything from aardvarks to Zionism in encyclopedias, dictionaries, atlases, statistics and business directories..... These books are SO important they can be used only in the LRC.

INFORMATION BOOKS

...arranged on the shelves by subject. Find the subject number you need by using the shelf guides and headings, subject index and catalogues. It's so easy!

FICTION BOOKS

...arranged in A-Z order of the author's last name. Look out for new collections of graphic novels, quick reads, biographies, short stories and picture pop-up books.....

CASSETTES

... or listen to your favourite stories, plays or poems on tape, learn a new language.....

VIDEOS

... and slide-packs to help with project work are kept at the Help Desk. Please ask!

Fig. 6.2 *Information about Cramlington Community High School's library*

Leaflets and guides to the library are useful if seen in the context of the use of the library for curricular purposes and not as an end in itself and it is important that pupils are encouraged to use the leaflet positively and that the leaflet/guide is referred to in subsequent visits to the library. Otherwise, library guides can end up as yet more unread pieces of paper collected by Year 1 pupils.

Library rules

Libraries of all kinds tend unfortunately to be associated with rules, often of a draconian and threatening nature, e.g. boldly stating in a leaflet seen by pupils on their first visit to the library that those who persistently break the rules will be banned from the library. In school libraries today, such approaches are very uncommon and school librarians often adopt the practice (referred to in Chapter 3) of seeking agreement amongst pupils about what the rules of the library should be. This may take the form of statements such as, 'We agree not to disturb others who are working in the library (or classroom); or, We agree not to raise our voices in the library (or classroom)', with the statements being prominently displayed in poster form around the school. Other approaches which stress the positive aspects of using the school library may be provided within the library guide and Figure 6.3 shows the guidance given to pupils at St Machar Academy.

Using the library catalogue

When pupils use the school library, they will be encouraged to make good use of the library catalogue. Many schools now have automated library systems and key word searching is one of the main benefits of such systems. Whether the school library has an automated catalogue or a card catalogue with a subject index, it is important that pupils using the catalogue view this process as one which follows the identification of key words or phrases relating to their topic. Pupils will also need to be reminded of the need to evaluate the results of a search of the catalogue. For example, a pupil searching an OPAC in a school library under a chosen key word and finding that their search results in over 50 'hits', will be encouraged to think about the implication of such a result, i.e. the actual time it would take to find and examine 50+ books or other resources.

NOW   -   Learn the LIBRARY CODE

L ibrary Club - Lots of Fun - Remember to buy your pass from the librarian.

I nformation - All around you - LOOK !   LISTEN !   LEARN !

B ehaviour is important.   The library is for all pupils to enjoy - DON'T you spoil it for others.

R eturn books on time.

A fter school - use the library - it's open 'till 4.30.

R ules are for KEEPING - not   BREAKING.

Y ou must be quiet at *ALL* times -   people are *STUDYING ! ! !*

C are for the books and tapes that you borrow.

O verdue books -   you will have to pay a *FINE ! ! !*

D on't **eat** or **drink** in the library - use the social areas for this.

E njoy reading -   it's **F U N**

Fig. 6.3 *A positive approach to rules at St Machar Academy*

This evaluation should result in the pupil narrowing the search which may mean going back to the topic and the key words identified originally in order to extend the key word map or list to include narrower terms or it may mean that the pupil should combine some of the key words to form a Boolean search which includes 'and', for instance Exports AND Cars AND Japan. Pupils will not find searching the catalogue difficult as a mechanical exercise but may find the skills of relating what was done in the classroom, i.e. the key word map or list, to use of the library catalogue more difficult. Figure 6.4 shows guidance given to pupils at Hinchingbrooke School in using the library's automated catalogue and linking this use to key word searching.

Using books and journals

Pupils who are using information resources in the secondary school for the first time may well need assistance in using books and journals, depending on their experiences in primary school. As with the introduction to the library, the process of showing pupils how the information in books and journals is constructed should not be overemphasized, nor should it take a long time. It is useful, however, for teachers and school librarians to reinforce skills such as using the contents page, blurb and index of books when pupils are carrying out assignment work. There is also a need to ensure that pupils, having identified key words in the classroom, searched the catalogue, found books on the shelves and are about to use the books, do in fact follow up their classroom work by using key words when searching the contents page or index. Wray and Lewis's research found that while pupils clearly understood the *theory* of using indices in books, they did not follow this knowledge through by actually practising these skills.[3] Thus as well as providing guidance such as that from the Effective Teaching and Learning Strategies Group in Figure 6.5 and from Webster's High School in Figure 6.6, teachers and school librarians should check, perhaps by observation in the library, whether pupils do use the skills needed. The most important use of books and journals comes when the relevant information is found and Chapters 6 and 7 will cover these aspects.

Keywords

If you want books on a certain subject, either Fiction or Non-Fiction
– Press C (for Search by Keyword simple) and this screen will appear:

```
Simple Keyword Search
Help - <F1> Start again - <F3> Begin Search - <F10>
Exit - <Esc>

Enter the keywords you want to look for:

[NUCLEAR POWER]        OR      [NUCLEAR ENERGY]
                       AND
[POLLUTION]            OR      [            ] ___
```

You may use * : eg FISH* will match FISH, FISHING, FISH FARMING

All the Resources in the Resource Centre have been given 'keywords'. These are familiar words we use to describe frequently used topics, to help you find all the information you need for a project

You may use up to four keywords for your search, but remember that if you use the OR instruction (ie type keywords next to each other), you will widen your search and find more resources, but if you use the AND instruction (i.e. type keywords underneath each other) you will narrow your search and find fewer resources.

When you have entered all your keywords press F10 and a list of resources which include those topics will appear on the screen.

This search would find a list of resources on **pollution** of the environment by **nuclear power** or **nuclear energy**.

If I had only wanted pollution by nuclear energy I would have entered **nuclear energy** and **pollution**.

Points to remember when using the database

• Always read the screen if you don't remember what to do next. There will be instructions to help you.

• A long list of resources is not always a sign of success. You will not have time to look at them all and some may not be very useful.

Think about making your keyword searches more specific by using the AND instruction

Fig. 6.4 *Using Hinchingbrooke School Library OPAC*

Using an Index

An index at the back of a book is an alphabetical list of key words, telling you which page numbers to look up for each word.

The index you have been given is from a book on Dinosaurs. Use it to answer the following questions.

1. On which page would you find information about the Ultrasaurus?
2. Which pages give you information about a dinosaur's lifespan?
3. On which page would you find an illustration of a dinosaur's tail?
4. Where would you find a dinosaur compared to a lizard?
5. a) On which pages would you find out about a dinosaur's senses?

   b) Which other key words are you told to look up to find further information on senses?

Index

Figures in bold refer to captions

Albertosaurus 24
Apatosaurus 11
armour 9, 15

Bactrosaurus 15
beak 8
blood 10-11
body size 11
bones 6,7, 10,11
brain 12, 16,

Chasmosaurus 6, 7
cheeks 8
claws 8
climate 2,3
colour 14,15
communication 16-17

Deinonychus 24
digestion 7
dinosaurs
  Age of 2,3,5
dinosaurs compared to
  flamingo 21
  frog 17
  monkey 17
  lizard 10, 17
  crocodile 19
  owl 10, 11
Diplodocus 23

eyes and hearing 16
Edmontosaurus 17
eggs 18-19
extinction 28-29
eyes and eyesight 12, 13,14

feet 7, 30
food 4, 6 8-9, 23
fossils 3, 5 6, 7 27-29

guts 7, 9

hands 8,9
head 8,9
horns 21
Hypselosaurus 18

Iguanodon 9

jaws 8

lifespan 22-23

man-eating dinosaurs 8,9 11,12
migration 26-27
muscles 6,6

nests 18,20
nostrils 13,16

Oviraptor 18

Pentaceratops 27
plant-eating dinosaurs 4,5,6 7,8 9,9
  four-footed 9
  long-necked 9,11
  two-footed 9,16
pterosaurus 4,5

scales 14
senses 6, 12-13
  (see also ears, eyes, nostrils)
size 22-23
skeletons 6, 22 24, 25-27
skin 6,6 10 14-15
skull 7, 16

tail 8,11
teeth 7, 11 21,30

Ultrasuarus 23

Velociraptor 10,11

young 19, 20-22

Fig. 6.5 *Using an index in Ross High, Preston Lodge and Musselburgh Grammar schools*

Country Profile

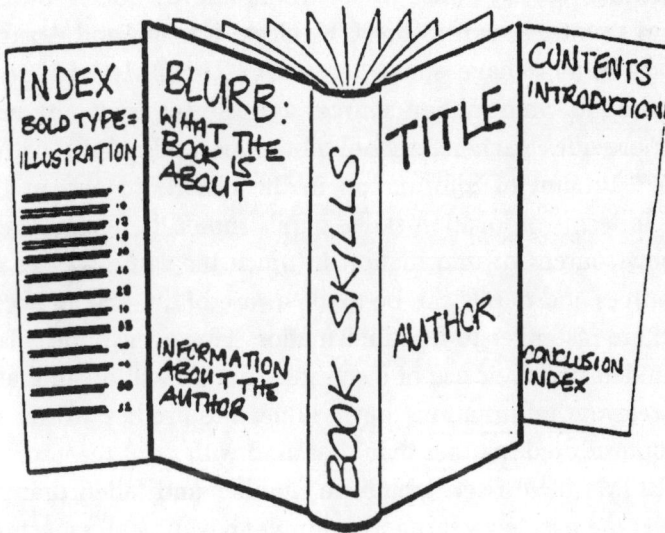

INDEX
BOLD TYPE=
ILLUSTRATION

BLURB:
WHAT THE
BOOK IS
ABOUT

INFORMATION
ABOUT THE
AUTHOR

BOOK SKILLS

TITLE

AUTHOR

CONTENTS
INTRODUCTION

CONCLUSION
INDEX

Book Skills

You will find most of the information for answering your **Key questions** in books.

Remember you do not need to start reading a book at page 1 to find out if it has the information you are needing.
Use the clues in the diagram above to find information quickly.

Make sure the book is up to date, check the book's date of publication – you will find this on the page opposite the Contents page.

If the book has the information you are looking for, write the title of the book, date of publication, author and publisher in your **Log sheet** (this will make it easier to write up the list of books used to compare your country profile).

Remember you can select and reject materials.
You don't have to use everything you find.

Don't hang on to materials that other people might be waiting to use.

Fig. 6.6 *Using books at Webster's High School*

Using electronic information sources

Although the pattern of use of electronic information resources is very erratic in countries such as the UK, USA, Canada and Australia, most secondary schools have some access to CD-ROMs whilst other have access to online information sources and the Internet. These electronic sources provide teachers, school librarians and pupils with a vastly increased amount of information in the classroom and in the school library. In terms of location skills, pupils should be encouraged to view these new sources of information in much the same way as they view print sources and pupils can be made aware of the ease of access to and use of these resources to find information. However, pupils also need to be reminded that their use of electronic sources will mean that, in order to find relevant information, they will need to use key words in an even more sophisticated manner than that used with print resources.

CD-ROMs have risen greatly in number and fallen dramatically in price over the past few years and examples covering all aspects of the secondary curriculum can be found. Figure 6.7 shows a list of the most highly recommended CD-ROMs chosen by teachers and school librarians for the now discontinued *School Library 2000* journal.[4]

There is therefore no shortage of available CD-ROMS and as the number in each school increases, pupils will have access to an even greater range of sources. This raises the question of how school librarians should make information about CD-ROMs available via the library cat-

---

The Arts: Great Artists; Microsoft Art Gallery; A Passion for Art; Microsoft Musical Instruments; The Musical World of Professor Piccolo.

Cross-curricular: The Complete Oxford English Dictionary; Grolier's Encyclopedia; The Louvre; The Way Things Work.

Reference: World Book Multimedia Encyclopedia; Encarta '96; DK World Reference Atlas; ECCTIS; The Times and Sunday Times CD-ROM.

Science: Redshift 2; Body Works 4.0; The Eyewitness Encyclopedia of Science; Forces and Effects; Compact Questions: Science.

Special Needs: My World 2 CD Extra; KidPiz Studio; Thinking Things; The Tortoise and the Hare; Treasure Chest.

Fig. 6.7 *Highly recommended CD-ROMs from School Library 2000*

alogue or OPAC. If pupils are going to use key words to retrieve information from CD-ROMs then teachers and school librarians can reinforce this process by providing access to information *about* CD-ROMs – what they contain, their scope and level – via the OPAC. In order to do this, school librarians in many schools now ask teachers to complete curriculum-related proformas on which key words used in the curriculum can be attached to entries in the catalogue for CD-ROMs in the same way as they are for books.

Pupils will not find the mechanics of using CD-ROMs difficult as they will be used to following instructions on screen. They will need guidance on the effective use of the CD-ROM, for specific topics in geography such as those shown in Figure 6.8 (overleaf) from Burntwood School and in Figure 6.9 (p.101) from Grange School.

While these two examples provide pupils with help on locating information on the CD-ROM, it should be noted that, in these cases, the *purpose* of finding this information is clearly established by the teacher and thus location is directly related to this purpose. Also, both are good examples of how guidance for pupils should be curriculum based and not based on hypothetical examples as so often seen in library guides or exercises for pupils. Also, in the case of the Grange School example, pupils were using this CD-ROM but were also using other CD-ROMs such as the York CD, a bank of photographs produced on the Pbase CD and Encarta '96. Pupils are also encouraged to use print sources within the same project. Martin (the teacher in the Grange School example) and Bailey argue that, 'Researching material requires enquiry skills: these must be developed before appropriate material can be selected and used to best effect. Research needs key ideas, structure, a knowledge of what resources are available and an ability to search and operate relevant systems. Selection techniques are needed; more than ever now that students can print out reams of material from a computer simply by clicking a mouse'.[5]

Year 8 – Researching Information Using a CD Rom
Infobook – Information Finder by World Book

In Geography you have been looking at the topic of 'Water'. This is an excellent topic to research using the CD Rom but it is obviously a vast topic and you will have to be selective about the information you use. This sheet will guide you through the most efficient way to search for the information *you need* about water.

At the first screen press ENTER to load the program

The screen will split into two windows:
• the **left** side contains the outline of the sections of related information found in the search.
• the **right** side contains the information
  (The first screen when the program loads always shows the information about the letter 'A')

At the top you can see the **'Enter search topic'** box – use your mouse to point and click in the box.

Type your key word: water
                          enter

Look at the message at the bottom of the screen
Article 1 of 34 (this means there is 34 different sections of information on Water)

Obviously you do not need all of this information. Scroll down the Outline (or use cursor keys) to see what sections are available. On the opposite side the text will correspond to highlighted title.
You should read the information on screen and make notes, if time does not allow you could print. Don't bother to print very short sections.

To Print: make sure the name of the relevant section to be printed is selected.
                 Select Print from the tool bar, **F9** gives you this choice

Print
Text in view
Section: ???
Entire Article (?? pages)
Article outline

This literally means the text on screen

This means the section which is currently highlighted on the left – check how long it is first

Check how many pages this is. **You must never print more than 3 pages without your IT teacher's permission.**

This is a print of the information in the outline

Think about what you really need
Select the option you require
Press **Enter** (this will print a copy almost immediately on the Dot Matrix printer)
If it does not print – check that the printer is on line.

To Quit Information Finder:
Click on: Functions (top menu bar)
                 Exit to DOS
                 YES
                 Enter

Fig. 6.8 *Using a CD-ROM for a geography project at Burntwood School*

Medieval Castles

The aim of this work is to find out about Medieval Castles. You are to find information about

- the names of medieval castles
- where the castles were built
- why they were built
- when they were built
- life in a medieval castle
- the castle design and its defences
- how to attack a castle
- when castles became less important

Load the **Medieval Realms CD.**

From the opening menu, choose **Search**. Choose Search by **Topic**
Now click on each of the topics to see which sub-topics has information about **castles**.
Click on it and choose **OK**. This will list all the items of data about castles.
Click on the item you want to see and click on **View Record**.
List takes you back to the list of items. **Picture** shows the picture on the full screen.
Text shows the text on full screen. **Both** shows text and picture at the same time.
G is a glossary of words, giving their meaning.

Activity

Choose one of the castles listed. Research information about it using all the items of information. Present your work on one page to include the following:

- Its name
- A sketch of the castle (one scene will do)
- When it was built
- Where it is and why it was built there
- The names of people who built it and lived there
- The castle site (the ground it was built on)
- The castle defences
- Important events in the castle's history
- What remains of the castle today

Activity

Choose one other castle. In what ways is this castle similar to the one you have already studied?
In what ways is this castle different from the one you have already studied.
Describe about five ways for each.

Fig. 6.9 *Using the* 'Medieval Realms' *CD-ROM at Grange School*

Using the Internet

A growing number of schools in the UK and other countries now have access to the Internet which can be used by pupils as a new, and potentially very relevant, source of information for project work. As noted in Chapter 2, the NCET's 'Libraries of the future' project found that accessing relevant information on the World Wide Web was often problematic for pupils in terms of the time taken and the amount of Websites found from even the most simple searches. One of the problems which schools in the UK, USA, Canada, Australia and elsewhere have identified is the access which pupils have to material which is not seen as suitable for secondary school pupils and this includes sexist, racist, political and pornographic material. However, there is little agreement on what is deemed suitable and this debate will continue. Schools which do have Internet access have developed Acceptable Use Policies (AUPs) which normally means that pupils and their parents or guardians have to sign a form stating that the Internet will only be used according to guidelines issued by the school. Such guidelines normally include statements such as that seen in Hinchingbrooke School under 'Internet search advice' (Figure 6.10). As more schools acquire access to the Internet, the problem of pupils finding vast amounts of information and not being able to select relevant material is likely to grow although more sophisticated search engines are being developed. Pupils using the Internet, even with better search engines, will still need to be taught how to structure their searches very carefully in order to maximize the relevance of what is found and minimize the amount of material located.

Using people as information resources

Teachers and school librarians often find that pupils will restrict their searches for information to easily identifiable resources in print and electronic form in both the classroom and the school library. In many cases, particularly for project work, people may be the most valuable information resources or more particularly, people may be the best *starting point* for finding information. Within the school, the school librarian is the information professional but, like most other librarians, they often face reluctance on the part of their users to ask questions directly. The reasons for this tend to range from an underestimation of the importance of the enquiry to an overestimation of what the school librarian will be con-

Not Only Books – the Internet cont...

We are happy for you to use this terminal, but we expect you to act responsibly. Please remember that we keep a log of every time you connect with the World Wide Web and every site that you visit because we are interested in finding out how useful the World Wide Web is.

Instructions on how to use the terminal are by the side of the computer. Read this carefully.

For more advice on Search techniques see the Librarians or Mr Grey.

This information is for your benefit. It is important.

You may expect to lose your chance to use our Internet facility if you do not follow this advice.

INTERNET SEARCH ADVICE

1. We expect you to use this facility in a responsible way.

2. Complete the form on the other side of this card before starting an Internet search. It will save you time, the school phone bills, and will be used to show how people use The Net.

3. Show the librarians this form and your library card before starting a Search.

4. Use Keywords to enter a query in Netsearch. Use Net Directory, a hotlist or Bookmarks to go to interesting places.

5. When searching for material ask yourself – 'Would i be happy to show this to my teacher or parent?' If the answer is no, you should not be looking at that material. Move on to a more suitable page immediately.

6. Don't hog the computer. 15 minutes online is maximum. Use that time to collect suitable pages and save them to disk for viewing later. Never waste Online time!

7. Return this card to the library counter when you've finished your session and show your library card again to 'log off'.

What is the address of the Hinchingbrooke Home page?

What is the school e-mail address?

What should you do if you find something unsuitable on The Net?

Fig. 6.10 *Guide to using the Internet at Hinchingbrooke School*

cerned with. In the first instance pupils do not ask because they have not thought through the consequences of not finding relevant information and in the second instance pupils think that the librarian will be shocked at being posed such an apparently simple enquiry. To overcome this reluctance on the part of the pupils, most school librarians stress the importance of asking the librarian in their library for literature. Figure 6.11 from Cramlington Community High School includes people within school and outside school as sources of information.

Conclusion

From the above it can be seen that while pupils do need the skills to locate information from a variety of information formats, many location skills are in fact mechanical and require very little guidance. What is more important is that pupils recognize location as part of the learning/research process which they follow when seeking information for a purpose. Thus any guidance given to pupils on using libraries in schools needs to be in the context of finding information, not for its own sake but for a particular curricular purpose. Also, it is important not to fall into the trap of some commercial publishers of library guides which use phrases such as 'Cracking the code', 'The library game', or 'The library mystery tour' which attempt to produce guidelines which can be used in all school libraries. The problem with such schemes is that each school library is (and should be) unique in some respects, often reflecting particular curricular themes and that generalized schemes may have *negative* effects on pupils' location skills because pupils will not see a direct curricular link and will tend to isolate these skills from actual project work. Thus finding information will not be problematic in itself but could, however, pose more problems for pupils in that they must then select what is relevant and be able to read what is found in a way which produces understanding, links with existing knowledge and information and ideas which relate to the purpose of the original search.

Teaching Plan

A class of 24 pupils in their fourth year of secondary school are being asked to complete an assignment in computer studies. Pupils have to choose a topic relating to an aspect of information technology and society, e.g. in industry, in services such as banking, in local or central government, in the home, at school. The format, length and marking criteria of the assignment have previously been explained to the pupils. Each lesson lasts 40 minutes.

INFORMATION SOURCES 7 RESOURCES

BOOKS	Fiction Books
	Information Books
	Reference Books
	Encylopedias
	Directories
	Maps
COMPUTERS	CD ROMS
	Multimedia
	Internet
	Software Disks
	Teletext
NEWSPAPERS & MAGAZINES	Daily/weekly
	Local/National
	Subject Specialist
	Cuttings Files
AUDIOVISUAL	Television
	Cassettes
	Radio
	Video
PEOPLE	Library Staff
	Teachers
	Family
	Friends
ORGANISATIONS	Community Groups
	Societies
	Businesses
	Public Library
	Museums
	Government/Council
	Advice Bureaux
OBJECTS	Leaflets
	Posters
	Photographs
	Slides
	Artefacts

IF IN DOUBT ....ASK!!

INFORMATION SOURCES 7 RESOURCES

- BOOKS
- COMPUTERS
- NEWSPAPERS 7 MAGAZINES
- AUDIOVISUAL
- PEOPLE
- ORGANISATIONS
- OBJECTS

IF IN DOUBT ....ASK!!

Fig. 6.11 *Reminding pupils that people are sources of information at Cramlington Community High School*

Lesson 2: Location

In this lesson, the class is split into two groups, with one half staying in the computer room with the teacher and working on a desk top publishing exercise and the other half going to the school library. This lesson is taught by the school librarian who was present at the introductory part of lesson 1.

1 Class enter, get settled and their assignments sheets, which have been commented on by the teacher and the school librarian, are returned (5 minutes).

2 The school librarian briefly explains that the aims of the lesson are to:

✔ remind pupils of the PLUS model

✔ remind pupils of the use of key words when searching the library's catalogue (OPAC)

✔ outline the information resources in the library relating to computer studies

✔ allow pupils an opportunity to use the CD-ROMs (three workstations available) (3 minutes).

3 Pupils are issued with a sheet on which they fill in their assignment title and make a list of key words to use. Pupils work in groups of three and, in turn, search the OPAC, look for books and journals on the shelves (and in the reserve section) and use the CD-ROMs to search national newspapers for information about their topic. Pupils are reminded to write down sources which they will include in their bibliography (25 minutes).

4 Pupils return to their seats and are reminded that this session is their *initial* search for information. The school librarian asks each group what difficulties, if any, they experienced when searching for information and comments on these (5 minutes).

5 The links between purpose and location are restated and pupils are told that, in the following lesson, they will be looking at good habits in reading for information (2 minutes).

References

1 School Curriculum and Assessment Authority, *Consultation on the National Curriculum*, SCAA, 1994.

2 Brown, J., 'Developing information skills', in Kinnell, M. (ed.), *Managing library resources in schools*, Library Association Publishing, 1994, 189–203.

3 Wray, D. and Lewis, M., 'Extending interactions with non-fiction texts: an EXIT into understanding', *Reading*, 29 (1), April 1995, 2–9.

4 *School library 2000*, Issue 11, May 1996, 22–5.

5 Martin, F. and Bailey, P., 'Evaluating and using resources', in *The geography teachers' handbook*, Geography Teacher's Association, 1995.

Chapter 7
Reading for information

After reading this chapter, you will be able to:

✔ **evaluate a range of reading strategies which pupils may use when reading for information**
✔ **understand how reading is linked to purpose in the information skills process**
✔ **examine methods of teaching pupils how to skim and scan information resources**
✔ **understand the importance of understanding when pupils read for information**
✔ **identify methods pupils may use to evaluate texts in print and electronic information resources.**

The steps of identifying purpose and location in the information skills process can be seen as leading up to the centre piece of the process, i.e. the use of information, ideas, concepts, theories and evidence available to pupils in the range of information sources available. Reading texts, whether on paper or on screen, lies at the heart of the information skills process because unless pupils can read effectively and understand what they read, then even if they have a clear purpose in mind and have found a range of sources relevant to their topic, they will not be able complete their project or assignment satisfactorily without further help. Despite a large number of research projects in aspects of information skills in the UK and elsewhere, there is still a lack of focus on this key aspect of the process by teachers and school librarians in secondary schools. Whether this is caused by a lack of knowledge of the skills involved and the possible methods of teaching such skills on the part of teachers and school librarians or whether it is caused by an *assumption* that, if pupils are in secondary school, they will be able to read for information using effective strategies, is unclear but anecdotal evidence suggests that it may be a mixture of both.

A further complicating factor in secondary schools is the compartmentalization of staff into fairly strict subject departments and it is assumed that the English department will necessarily deal with 'reading'. While it will be true that English teachers will focus on reading, e.g. how to read a Shakespeare play or a poem by Seamus Heaney or a novel by Robert Westall, they will not necessarily focus on how to adopt different reading strategies when reading about the climate of a country or a contemporary report from World War 1 or an essay on world poverty. Millard reinforces this point by arguing that:

> To be effective readers of non-fiction, children will need to develop very different skills from those associated with reading narrative. The chronological structure of the former leads the child to read continuously, moving from the opening of a story to its ending in a methodical and concentrated linear path... The skills needed to make good use of information texts is almost diametrically opposed to the process of concentrated absorption which is appropriate to the reading of fiction.[1]

While most primary/elementary schools have reading policies, most secondary/high schools do not have a policy for reading which covers all areas of the curriculum. The result for those pupils who are less adept at reading than their peers is that, while the history teacher cannot or does not teach pupils how to read historical documents or accounts, the same teacher will *expect* pupils to be able to do this and indeed will *evaluate* the pupils' ability to read and understand when marking the project or assignment.

This chapter seeks to redress some of the balance by referring to contemporary research such as that of Wray and to reinforce some of the ideas propounded by Irving and Tabberer in the 1980s in relation to reading for information. The chapter will examine reading strategies, linking reading to purpose, skimming and scanning, reading and understanding, and evaluation of texts. Examples from schools will be provided where appropriate.

Reading strategies

Wray and Lewis's evidence shows that pupils will adopt different strategies when reading for different purposes, e.g. looking for a telephone number, reading the sports pages of a daily newspaper or reading a chapter in a textbook. The authors argue that the extent to which pupils' reading will be effective will depend on whether pupils take 'appropriate and conscious decisions about which reading strategy to adopt in which circumstances and when to switch strategies'. Wray and Lewis argue that teachers could help pupils by showing them, in the context of the curriculum, a range of different approaches to different information sources and importantly, to explain to pupils why the *teacher* might adopt a particular strategy when reading a particular source. There was little evidence of teachers using their own experience of reading as the basis for encouraging pupils to adopt similar strategies.[2]

Irving supports the views of Wray and Lewis, stating that pupils should be introduced to a range of strategies to help them identify the approach which suits them best.[3] Thus it can be seen that just as pupils learn differently, as seen in Chapter 1, they may also prefer different strategies for reading. The key issue here is whether pupils are given the opportunity to examine the different strategies which they might adopt and whether they are made aware of the importance of this self-assessment by teachers and school librarians who are presenting them with topics to research and a range of different information resources which will satisfy the research needs.

Interacting with the text

Wray and Lewis focus specifically on how pupils interact with text and state that while the stages of identifying purpose, locating sources and examining reading strategies are important 'it is the stage of interacting with the text which remains at the heart of the process'.

What occurs when pupils read for information is a transaction between the pupil and the text which is based on the pupil's existing knowledge of the topic and 'the intended message of the author of the text'.

Pupils can then be encouraged to examine how different texts are constructed by using techniques such as identifying the sequence of the text, restructuring text to increase understanding and highlighting text to identify what is relevant and what should be ignored.[4] Claxton uses similar terminology to Wray and Lewis, stating that successful pupils 'seem to adopt a stance of active interaction with the topic'.

Claxton points out that pupils often demonstrate this kind of interaction when watching television programmes by examining what is happening in a film and how it relates to the rest of the film or to what they have seen in other films, but do not transfer this approach to school work. Claxton argues that pupils will often have to adopt strategies of re-reading difficult sections of text. Like Wray and Lewis, Claxton emphasizes that, 'Like all learning strategies, however, these need to be practised and encouraged, so that a learner can build up the ability and the confidence to use them'.[5]

Linking reading to purpose

Irving argues that reading will be most effective when related to purpose and states that, 'Without a clear purpose, pupils will tend to read unselectively and make voluminous, unstructured notes'.[6]

Wray and Lewis also focus on the need to link reading to an identified purpose and refer to the work of Brown whose research found that successful readers were conscious of their own reading strategy and that this involved:

✔ clarifying one's purposes for reading, that is understanding the explicit and implicit demands of a particular task
✔ identifying the important aspects of a text
✔ focusing attention on these principal aspects rather than on relatively trivial aspects
✔ monitoring on-going activities to determine whether comprehension is taking place
✔ engaging in self questioning to check whether the aims are being achieved
✔ taking corrective action if and when failures in comprehension are detected.

Reading for meaning

Wray and Lewis's research has shown that if pupils are to be engaged in 'reading for meaning' then pupils will need to be encouraged to monitor their own understanding of a text by using what the authors refer to as 'debugging skills'. If a pupil does not understand an idea or concept or explanation in a particular piece of text, then various strategies can be adopted: keep reading and hope that the author will explain, re-read the passage, or seek help either by using a dictionary to look up the meaning of a word or by asking a suitable person. Some pupils will be much better at handling problems in comprehension than others and Wray and Lewis argue that those pupils who are not adept at handling comprehension problems can be taught strategies to cope with such problems. Strategies will include the need for pupils to recognize the purpose of their reading and determine whether a comprehension problem is important in relation to that purpose. For example, pupils searching for information on examples of the effects of earthquakes in geography may not need to understand all the technical terms used in order to find relevant information, whereas pupils reading for information about gravity in physics *will* need to understand terminology and consult the teacher or school librarian if problems occur. Wray and Lewis conclude that, 'As with the adoption of an appropriate reading strategy, we suggest that the most effective teaching strategy for this is for teachers actively to demonstrate to children their own thinking/monitoring processes as they try to understand a text'.[7]

The work of Wray and Lewis should be seen as important by teachers in all subjects and by school librarians as it represents a new approach to reading for information and provides a model which, if followed up in schools, could see marked improvements in pupils' approaches to using information resources.

Skimming and scanning

The government guidelines for English teaching *English for ages 5 to 16* stress that at Key Stage 2 (upper primary/elementary school) pupils should be taught 'how to read for different purposes, adopting appropriate strategies for the task. The strategies should include skimming to gain an overall impression of the text and scanning to locate a specific piece of information.[8]

Millard argues that, 'Information books need to be quickly surveyed for their relevance to the information required, using textual structural pointers like contents pages, indexes, chapter headings and subheadings, glossaries and even the place and date of publication. Children need experience in skimming for general impressions and scanning to locate specific details in the book'.[9]

Examples from schools

When reading for information, pupils can be taught a variety of strategies which will make them more efficient and effective readers and skimming and scanning skills are recognized as being of particular use when pupils are using information resources of different kinds. Skimming can be used by pupils who want to evaluate the usefulness of a particular book, chapter of a book, journal article, newspaper or section of a CD-ROM. It is important that pupils have a purpose in both skimming and scanning and can learn to use key words when first using information resources. Figure 7.1 shows advice given to pupils in Anderson High School's 'Study skills module'.

Pupils can be encouraged to learn that, with certain information resources which they locate, they do not need to read in depth in order to quickly evaluate the potential usefulness of a printed or electronic text. Figure 7.2 shows the guidance and practice given by teachers and school librarians in Ross High, Preston Lodge and Musselburgh Grammar schools. This approach which suggests to pupils the idea of 'searching for clues' provides an appropriate link to the importance of reading with a purpose.

What you can do is look over a passage *before* you read it. Glance through it looking for important information. Before you begin reading it properly, look at the paragraph headings and any diagrams (since they are good at summarising information). Once you have done that, you will have some idea what the passage is about and this will help you understand it.

The above process is known as *skimming*. It means glancing through a passage looking for any important information.

What is being suggested is that you *skim* an article (book, magazine, chapter, set of questions) *before* you begin to read it properly.

Fig. 7.1 *Guidance on skimming for Anderson High School pupils*

Pupils' Notes – Section 1 – Topic 3

<u>Locating Information</u>

<u>Reasons for Reading</u>

<u>Skimming</u>

Skimming means reading a passage very quickly to get a general idea of what it is about.

You can also skim through a book looking at the title, the list of contents and chapter headings. You are <u>searching for clues</u> as to what the book is about. Skimming saves time when you are searching for information.

Skim this passage as quickly as you can. Get someone to time you. You should only take about 15 seconds!

<u>Passage 1</u>

Over the past fifty years, pollution has become a major problem for Scotland. Pollution chokes rivers, destroys life in the iceans, poisons the air and spoils the land. Mankind is responsible for this destruction of the environment. The use of chemical fertilisers, uncontrolled release of industrial waste and oil spillages all contribute to the problem in Scotland. We are all responsible. We must act now to preserve the natural treasures of Scotland for future generations.

<u>Instructions</u>

Without looking back on the passage, decide what it was about.

Was it about

       (a) - oil slicks?
       (b) - pollution?
       (c) - Scotland?
       (d) - pollution in Scotland?

Write down the letter of your choice of answer

Fig. 7.2   *An exercise in skimming for Ross High, Preston Lodge and Musselburgh Grammar school pupils*

Figure 7.3 is taken from *Keywords and learning* and emphasizes the point that skimming is intended to allow pupils to *save* time by adopting this strategy.

READING WITH A PURPOSE

SKIMMING

Purpose	–	when you want to get the "flavour" of the book or passage
	–	to help you decide whether to read it
	–	to help you decide how you should read it

How

SKIMMING IS FAST!

Let your eyes move <u>QUICKLY</u> over the main headings and keywords.

Don't waste time reading everything – you only need to get the "flavour"

If it's a BOOK – skim the TITLE
– skim the chapter headings
(look for a contents page to help you)

If it's a short PASSAGE – skim the TITLE
– skim the FIRST SENTENCE in each paragraph.

Fig. 7.3 *The purpose of skimming – from* Keywords and learning

Figure 7.4 is an extract from Oakham School's 'General Studies: optimizing your performance' and shows pupils the benefits of skimming texts and also what decisions they might make as a result of effective skimming.

Skimming allows you to:
Read a minimum amount of text
Gain the maximum amount of information from it
In the shortest possible time
Skimming material in this way you will have three choices:
Decide that the publication is not suitable
Decide that certain sections are appropriate to your needs
Decide that you need to read all of it. Even if this is the case your skimming has still been useful as it has given you an overview of the material

Fig. 7.4 *Benefits of skimming for pupils of Oakham School*

In the teachers' notes for Webster's High School's 'Country Profile' project (Figure 7.5), the use of a text's structure is encouraged and as in the Oakham School example, possible outcomes are noted.

Skimming

Involves looking quickly through a publication to familiarize yourself with its content.

Procedure:

Get pupils to summarize a book within three minutes!

This can be done by checking: the contents
                                                 introduction
                                                 headings
                                                 diagrams/photographs
                                                 maps
                                                 etc.

A tourist brochure could be skimmed to see if it has material relevant to the country profile.

After skimming, the pupil may decide that the publication is not suitable or that it does contain some useful information.

Fig. 7.5 *Teachers' notes for skimming exercises in Webster's High School*

Scanning

Scanning texts enables pupils to examine the information they have found and directly use the key words they identified when establishing their purpose to locate information or ideas which are relevant to their topic. Scanning, therefore, is a much more concentrated task than skimming and, in many cases, may follow the skimming of texts in a book or on a screen when using a CD-ROM. Irving states that scanning relates to what the reader *knows* is being looked for and the reader will scan pages or screens of text until key words or phrases which have been identified earlier have been found. Irving argues that, 'With both scanning and skimming, the main purpose is to utilise the text in as pragmatic a way as possible and with a minimum of time and effort'.[10]

Figure 7.6 from *Keywords and learning* encourages pupils to think about scanning in the context of specific information linked to a key word or phrase.

SCANNING

Purpose – when you are looking for <u>SPECIFIC INFORMATION</u> (e.g. a telephone number).

How

SCANNING IS FAST!

You should have a <u>specific KEYWORD</u> to look for. For example, when you are looking for a telephone number your keyword might be a person's NAME.

Run your eyes <u>QUICKLY</u> over the page,
or down the list, looking
for the keyword. Ignore
everything except your keyword.

Find the keyword and you've found the information you need!

57

Fig. 7.6 *Guidance on scanning from* Keywords and learning

Figure 7.7 from Ross High, Preston Lodge and Musselburgh Grammar schools tries to explain the importance of scanning. In the teachers' notes, the authors state that teachers and school librarians should remind pupils that they do not need to 'plough through the text' each time they are engaged in a reading for information task but that they should learn to use scanning to find information quickly.

Scanning

<u>Important</u>

When we **scan** for information, we are looking for certain **key words**.
We can **scan** a passage, a list, a table, an index – in fact any piece of written information.
Remember –
Scanning is hunting for **key words** or **key symbols**.
On the next page you will be given a number of keywords and a passage of text.
Scan the passage of text, noting down the numbers of lines in which the key words appear. The key words may appear more than once.

Fig. 7.7 *The importance of scanning for pupils of Ross High, Preston Lodge and Musselburgh Grammar schools*

Evaluation of texts

Wray and Lewis classify 'evaluating information' as a separate step in the information skills process and argue that, given the exponential growth of information in a range of forms, 'It seems even more important that we try to develop in children a questioning attitude to what they read'.

The authors state that readers should have control over what they read in that they are aware of contexts, e.g. cultural, political, historical, which affect the content of texts and that readers should be able choose what they read and they contrast this with the fact that, 'Propaganda and publicity rely for their effect upon recipients' lack of autonomy, and their sometimes overpowering influence upon the choices made'.

Pupils using information sources, Wray and Lewis continue, will have to be made aware of possible errors or bias within these sources and how to use techniques to spot these. The authors suggest that teachers 'deliberately confront children with examples of out of date, biased or contradictory written material and encourage them to discuss these features explicitly' and that teachers (following earlier examples) can demonstrate to pupils how they themselves evaluate data found in information resources.[11]

Evaluating Internet information

For teachers and school librarians, the present and future use of the Internet presents a huge challenge in evaluating information because of the existence of so many sites which are set up to propagate particular viewpoints on issues. Thus commercial companies such as banks, computer firms and soft drink manufacturers will all have websites which pupils can use for project work and which can provide much valuable information. However, the information provided is not free from bias. Similarly, many environmental groups have their own websites which often have detailed figures on, for example, the earth's climate but the information is presented from the viewpoint of that group and is therefore not unbiased. This problem of detecting bias is not new as pupils will have used sources such as politically-oriented newspapers in the past, but the Internet has increased greatly the *amount* of potentially biased information.

Figure 7.8 from Hinchingbrooke School provides pupils with some guidance on questions to ask when evaluating sources within a project on disasters.

EVALUATING YOUR EVIDENCE
Sometimes evidence is unclear or it contradicts something else you've found. **You must make the decision as to what is the truth. Discuss what you have found with your partner. Do you both agree on what is the most important evidence?

**Check the reliability of your source.
Does your information come from an expert? (How would you know?)
Is the information up to date? (Where would you find out?)

**Remember that some media are better than others at giving facts, details and opinion.

Fig. 7.8 *Evaluating sources at Hinchingbrooke School*

Conclusion

Reading for information presents pupils with a number of difficulties in terms of the structure of texts, the language used, the inclusion of visual or graphical material and the problems in selecting relevant information or ideas from the text. Reading for information includes the skills which pupils need to use both print and electronic sources and may include listening and viewing when using multimedia CD-ROMs. For teachers and school librarians, reading for information presents problems in terms of identifying what skills pupils already possess, knowing where similar skills are taught in other parts of the curriculum and being aware of the need to alert pupils to evaluation strategies when reading different kinds of texts. The need for reading strategies to be part of or linked to whole school information skills policies is evident but there are difficulties in planning and implementing such strategies across the curriculum in terms of planning the strategy, providing time for INSET and evaluating the outcomes of a reading for information strategy.

Because reading for information is so important to the information skills process in secondary schools, there is an obvious need for teachers and for school librarians in particular to re-evaluate their present information skills programmes to examine whether enough attention is given to reading for information or whether it is assumed that pupils will already have these skills and can transfer them across the curriculum. Present evidence shows that pupils may have *some* experience of these skills but that they do not necessarily transfer them across subject areas within the school.

Teaching Plan

A class of 24 pupils in their fourth year of secondary school are being asked to complete an assignment in computer studies. Pupils have to choose a topic relating to an aspect of information technology and society, e.g. in industry, in services such as banking, in local or central government, in the home, at school. The format, length and marking criteria of the assignment have previously been explained to the pupils. Each lesson lasts 40 minutes.

Lesson 3: Reading for information

1 Class enter, get settled and are given a sheet with a two-paragraph passage from a book on 'IT and society' (permission to reprint has been given) on one side and an alphabetical list of the pupils' assignment topics on the other (5 minutes).
2 The teacher briefly explains that the aims of the lesson are to:

   ✔ remind pupils of the PLUS model
   ✔ give pupils a short exercise in skimming
   ✔ allow pupils to see how information in books can be read in different ways
   ✔ give pupils an exercise in scanning (5 minutes).

3 Pupils are asked to read the passage, turn the paper over and then write down the key points of the passage. They then compare their findings in groups of four. The teacher explains how she would read the passage and what would help her to remember key points. Pupils are asked how *they* read the passage (10 minutes).
4 Pupils are then asked to restructure the text to see how the passage could be written in a different way but with the same meaning. The teacher gives pupils hints on how this might be done and some exam-

ples of pupils' work are commented on by the teacher after the pupils work in groups of four to complete this task (10 minutes).

5 Pupils are asked to scan the list and pick out the topics being studied by their group. The importance of scanning is reinforced by the teacher (5 minutes).

6 The teacher sums up the key points in reading for information and pupils are asked to select an article from a newspaper and make some notes on the article. They should then bring the notes to the class next week. Pupils leave (5 minutes).

References

1 Millard, E., *Developing readers in the middle years*, Open University Press, 1994.

2 Wray, D. and Lewis, M., 'Extending interactions with non-fiction texts: an EXIT to understanding', *Reading*, **29** (1), April 1995, 2–9.

3 Irving, A., *Study and information skills across the curriculum*, Heinemann, 1985.

4 Wray, D. and Lewis, M., op cit.

5 Claxton, G., *Teaching to learn*, Cassell, 1990.

6 Irving, A., op cit.

7 Wray, D. and Lewis, M., op cit.

8 Department for Education, *English for ages 5–16*, Department for Education, 1993.

9 Millard, E., op cit.

10 Irving, A., op cit.

11 Wray, D. and Lewis, M., op cit.

Chapter 8
Note taking

After reading this chapter, you will be able to:

✔ **understand the purpose of note taking in schools**
✔ **identify the links between note taking and original purpose for pupils**
✔ **evaluate the methods used by pupils to select and reject
information and ideas in information resources**
✔ **identify a range of techniques which can be used in note
taking.**

Once pupils have located appropriate sources of information and ideas
and have read, viewed or listened to sections of information resources,
they will take notes to provide them with the basis for their written assignment and will then translate these notes into a narrative form within their
assignment. Note taking is a key logistical step in the production of the
pupil's finished product and the quality of that finished product, whether
it be an essay, a report or an oral presentation, will to some extent depend
on the quality and quantity of notes taken. The quality of the notes will
reflect the pupil's understanding of what they have read and the quantity
of notes will reflect the pupil's ability to select and reject ideas and information found within texts of different kinds. Thus if a pupil is writing an
assignment which is not to be more than 1500 words long but takes notes
which constitute 3000 words, the pupil is not selecting in an efficient manner. As with all aspects of learning, individual styles will differ and each
of us will take notes in a slightly different format because the way we write
notes tends to express the way we, as individuals, read and interact with
texts. Thus an individual's notes will conceal hidden messages because of
the way they are written or structured and this is the reason why it is dif-

ficult for pupils to read each other's notes. Notes also trigger memory and when we read our own notes, it prompts us to recall more of the texts we have read or viewed and thus enables us to make more of our own notes than we could make of someone else's.

This chapter will examine the reasons pupils take notes in school, the links between note taking and purpose, the selection and rejection of information and ideas and the techniques used in note taking. Examples of schools will be provided where appropriate.

The context of note taking

In secondary schools, pupils take notes in a variety of contexts. Within the classroom, they may take notes while a teacher makes an introduction to a topic. This may involve noting the main points of what the teacher says about, for example, the political system of the USA in a modern studies class, as well as noting down points which the teacher writes on the black board or displays on an overhead projector (OHP). Another teacher may well present pupils with notes which the *teacher* has taken in order to provide pupils with supplementary material. In other contexts, for example in the school library, pupils will take notes from books, journals or CD-ROMs to form the basis of project work and the final project is likely to include a combination of the two types of notes – the classroom notes for a broadbrush understanding of the topic and information resource based notes to provide deeper exploration of the topic and examples related to the topic. Thus pupils doing assignment work on the UK and USA political systems may be introduced to the differences between Parliament and Congress in the classroom but may then use Encarta '96 for more detailed information on the two systems.

The purpose of note taking

Tabberer's research showed that when asked to classify the purposes of note taking, teachers identified a number of different purposes including:

✔ to create a record useful for a later examination
✔ to create a record for short term storage (e.g. to prepare for an essay)
✔ to get down important points regardless of later use, merely to help someone listen and concentrate

✔ to help to bring about an active reinterpretation of what is heard or seen
✔ to act as a brief reminder or *aide-memoir*
✔ to serve as the basis for extensive new notes or broader reading.[1]

Howe argues that one of the key purposes of note taking is to encourage pupils to pay attention to what they are reading and states that, 'It is by no means always easy to give sustained attention to information to be learned, especially when it is difficult'.

Thus the process of note taking, of the pupil writing the material in his or her own words, helps the material to become clear and meaningful to the pupil. Howe also states that where pupils pay close attention to texts by taking notes, then the input stage of information processing (see Chapter 1) will lead to better recall by the pupil and that 'the particular ways in which individuals direct their note taking activities have powerful effects in determining what is actually learned'.[2]

Selmes urges teachers to explain to pupils that 'Notes are important to make because they are a storage mechanism for facts, ideas, theories, relationships, experiments, experiences and views, so that they can be used later' and Selmes refers to pupils in his study as stating that once they understood the purposes and techniques of note taking, they felt that they had more control of their work and could achieve better results. Selmes produced an outline which teachers might use to explain to pupils the key purposes of note taking in school and this is shown in Figure 8.1.[3]

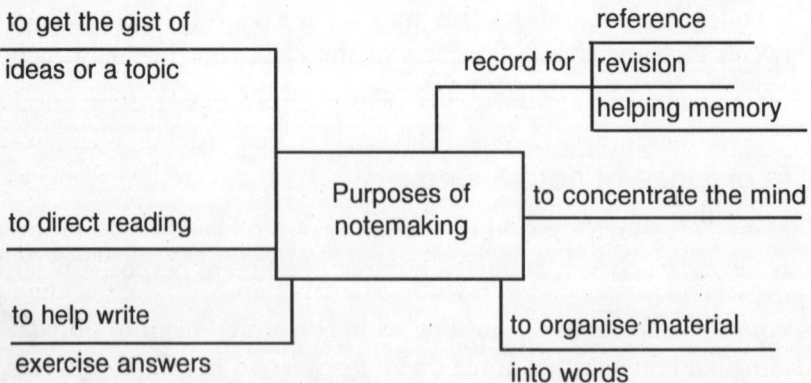

to get the gist of
ideas or a topic

record for | reference
revision
helping memory

Purposes of notemaking

to direct reading

to concentrate the mind

to help write
exercise answers

to organise material
into words

Fig. 8.1 *The purpose of note taking – from* Improving Study Skills

Wray and Lewis argue that one of the purposes of note making is to produce effective reading strategies for pupils, in that if pupils can read for information and demonstrate understanding from their reading in the form of a written piece of work, then note taking will be an intervening step in this process. The authors note that in higher education, students are often given no guidance in recording information and that, 'There is a strong argument for the teaching of these strategies, especially note-making, early on in children's careers'.[4]

A limited, unpublished survey by this author of Year 1 students entering higher education on a range of business studies, information management and healthcare courses, showed that very few students could remember being given written guidance on note taking in the last two years of secondary school.

Note taking and purpose

One of the problems faced by teachers and school librarians in relation to note taking, particularly in a school library where pupils are using a range of information sources, is that pupils often engage on note taking without having a clear purpose in mind when taking notes. The results tend to be that pupils either: take too many notes in an attempt to cover all possibilities when they come to write up their assignment; take too few notes because they are uncertain about what is relevant to them; copy out sections of printed material, or download sections from a CD-ROM or the Internet, perhaps hoping that this material will not be noticed by the teacher. To overcome this problem, it is important that pupils recognize note taking as a part of the information skills process which focuses first-ly on the concept of purpose. If pupils have a clear purpose in mind and have explored this purpose through concept maps and the identification of key words, then they can use this purpose and these key words as the basis for their note taking.

Wray and Lewis state that one of the key principles related to devel-oping teaching strategies in relation to interaction with texts is 'the need to consider information recording as inextricably linked to purpose for reading' and they further argue that if teachers do not clarify this link, by giving pupils examples of note taking related to purpose, then pupils may feel that they have to note down all points made in a particular passage and the dangers of copying are then greatly increased.[5] Howe argues that what pupils learn from notes will be influenced by the ways in which the notes were taken and that if pupils can learn to take 'better' notes then they will be able to make better use of them. Howe's definition of 'better' notes includes notes which are clearly structured and which are taken in relation to a set purpose, e.g. a list of topic questions which has been identified earlier and which the pupil seeks to answer through reading.[6]

Williams and Herring in *Keywords and learning* encouraged pupils to undertake 'Notemaking with a purpose' in an attempt to show pupils how to base their note taking around key words and then write their notes under these key word headings. Pupils, in the process of reading about a topic, will often discover new information or ideas about that topic which can help them both to understand the topic and also to introduce new aspects to their final assignment. Williams and Herring urged pupils to, 'Use main (more general) keywords and phrases as headings for your notes as you find information. Add keywords for the 'new' information to your map. Think about how it fits in with what you already know. Think about the connections and links between the bits of information you find'.[7]

Figure 8.2 from Hinchingbrooke School produces a leaflet entitled 'Note taking: five rules' for pupils. Figure 8.2 shows the first rule.

A: THE NOTES SHOULD BE RELEVANT

The notes you make should have something to do with the project you are working on. The facts and information you are collecting in note form should help you to answer the problem or questions you have set yourself in your project. It would therefore be a good idea to have a question or series of questions in mind even before you start to takes notes from a particular section of a book. You could write the question at the top of your notepaper to act as a constant reminder.

Fig. 8.2 *Note taking rules for pupils of Hinchingbrooke School*

Selection and rejection

Tabberer states that 'note-making is a process of selecting information, of making decisions or choices about what to keep and what to reject' and his project produced a model, in the form of a ladder, which might help pupils to improve their note taking through a series of exercises. Tabberer argues that, by using a series of simple then more complex exercises within the curriculum, pupils will develop a habit of note taking and become more confident of taking their own notes as opposed to relying on the teacher to produce notes for them. A simple exercise from Tabberer's project was based on pupils listening to a short passage on tape and writing down notes on the following question: 'If you had to choose one word to give someone else an ideas of what you've just heard, what would it be? Why? What other words would give a bit more help?'

A more complex task could be offered to more experienced note takers such as: 'Read chapter 7 and, together with the main points we have discussed in the video programme, produce some diagrammed notes on the crucial points'.[8]

Within these exercises, pupils would be expected to concentrate on increasingly broad questions but, with their experience of earlier note taking sessions in which they would learn to focus on the questions and, therefore, reject information or ideas which did not fit in with these questions, they would learn to cope with wider questions.

Claxton relates note taking to effective reading for information and argues that, in order to select and reject information, pupils must balance what they already know with what they do not know. In some cases, Claxton argues, pupils may have to re-read passages which contain difficult language or ideas before deciding on selection or rejection.[9]

The 'Trash and treasure' model

A recent discussion on the listserv BigSix, in which listserv members discuss aspects of information skills, the Internet and use of information resources in schools across the world, highlighted the importance of the selection and rejection principle in note taking. In some USA schools, students in the final years of elementary and the early years of high school were introduced to the concept of 'Trash and treasure' in note taking. Examples from the discussion included:

For the trash and treasure . . . I copied paragraphs from a non fiction book which the kids were studying. They had to search the paragraphs for answers to questions. The words that answered the question were treasure words, and were circled. The other words were trash and were drawn through.

Basically it [Trash and treasure] begins with highlighting on print (I had the kids use yellow crayon) the words which contain the essential facts – the treasure words. From there the kids move on to taking the treasure words and putting them into their own words.[10]

Note taking techniques

As was noted above, pupils will develop their own individual styles of note taking which they alone can fully interpret. However, some pupils are undoubtedly more efficient at taking and making effective use of notes than others. The most successful pupils will need little guidance on taking notes as they will perceive note taking as a logical progression from reading and towards writing. Other pupils will need much more help for a variety of reasons which include a lack of planning, a lack of understanding, a surfeit of information and a lack of knowledge of different techniques which can be applied.

Note taking frames

Wray and Lewis note that 'although skilful adult note-takers might well develop their own note structures to fit particular purposes and texts, younger students will need their initial attempts at note-making quite heavily scaffolded by structures suggested by their teachers'.

The authors used some of these structures, in the form of grids and frames, with pupils and found that there is 'some evidence that children can begin to make their own decisions about note-making as they see for themselves the usefulness of guiding structures'.[11]

Figure 8.3 shows an example of the use of Wray and Lewis's frames in a geography project done by special needs pupils at Alleyne's High School. The teachers found that the use of frames greatly improved the pupils' note taking (and subsequently writing) skills. The reasons for this improvement included the support which the frames gave to pupils when thinking about their topic and how they should use geographical terminology when responding to the questions in the frames. The frames also gave pupils more confidence in their own ability and served to motivate the pupils. Figure 8.4 shows how the same pupil's work (as shown in Figure 8.3) improved as a result of using the frames.

What most surprised me about photo B was

The thing that mot surprised me was that theire was a lorry going up redford Street if it was a Sunday because firms are closed on Sundays.

What most surprised the person I spoke to was

That theire wasn't many people around. That everybody who took part knew a lot more information because most people live or shop in Stone.

They found out the same things as me. For example.

double yellow lines, all of the Natural Factors. The jobs which were publican, waitress, heirdressers, Postmen, post office workers, lorry drivers and the council. It might be a sunday and the who decides section.

We found out different things.
For example

nobody mentioned the dentist.

Fig. 8.3 *Note taking frame used by pupils of Alleyne's High School*

Images of Nairobi

I was in the group that looked at the photos numbered
2, 4, 6, 9, 11, 13

We found the photos interesting for several reasons.
Because it's a lot similre to England because theires
mosques in Secke and Longton, Esso garages
everywhere. theire's a Hotel (the Hyatt regency) next
to the international convention centre that has
windows like the one in Nairobi and the homes are the
same.

We discovered that
Education is important over theire like in England
because you can see Mrs Obard's son and daughter
doing homework and in her office all of the work is in
English.

We also learnt that
It was very much like England in the way that they
have lap top computers and everything is like outs.
They call kenya a developing country and England a
developed country but in some ways theires looks
richer than England.

Finally it was very interesting that
A large amount of the population were moslims as we
can see in picture 9. The mosque is full of them and
theire is lots outside. so you can see this because the
mosque is big.

Fig. 8.4 *Improvement in depth in pupil's note taking following the use of
note taking frame at Alleyne's High School*

Note taking grids

The discussion on note taking on the BigSix listserv referred to above also included references to grids which were used by teachers and school librarians (library media specialists) in the USA. Some of the messages sent included:

> For the data charts, I got this idea from a workshop . . . and it works well. Take a big piece of drawing paper and fold it in half four times. This gives you lots of little squares. Across the top, write the information you want them [the pupils] to find. For example, if they were studying a planet, they might write size, distance from the sun, temperature range and number of moons. On the left side of the paper, going down, write the names of the sources you want them to use, for example, Compton's CD. They then write the information in the square under the topic and on the same line as the source they got it from. Writing in squares seems to automatically make them paraphrase and shorten what they write and we almost never have problems with kids copying from a book.

> We put the grid on butcher paper. On the left hand column, we list the sources students are to use. At the top, running to the right, we list the questions. This is so manageable and concrete for these students. Below is an example:

Source	Did they Exist?	What does warm-blooded mean?	What makes scientists think they were warm-blooded?
New Book of Knowledge			
Internet			
Warm-Blooded Dinosaurs			

> As you can see it's a wonderful method. Each question is answered by word or phrase from each source. Then the student can immediately see there might be different information from different sources. Students put all the words and phrases into a conclusion for each question.[12]

Within schools, a number of examples of guidance given to pupils on taking notes can be found and this guidance comes in the form of reminding pupils of the questions they should ask when taking notes, the form of notes they might take and what to avoid when note taking. Figure 8.5 is taken from Lothian Region's guidelines to senior pupils.

Before you start a piece of research you must plan what you are going to do. That means deciding what has to be done – which resources might be useful, where to find them, and how best to use the sources of information.

Ask yourself the following questions:

What should I make a record of?
What is important?
What is relevant?
How could I record it? . . . notes, diagrams, photocopying . . .

Make notes as you read
Notes are to help you remember what information you should use.

Remember . . .
- note down the details of the resource for your bibliography
- note words to look up in a dictionary
- list keywords and headings
- do not copy straight from the text.

Fig. 8.5 *Advice on note taking from Lothian Region School Library Service*

Figure 8.6 is part of the information skills booklets given to pupils from Ross High, Preston Lodge and Musselburgh Grammar schools and is included in a section which outlines the ways pupils can record information, e.g. spider diagrams, tree diagrams, flow charts, time lines, hierarchies, bar graphs and matrices.

A REMINDER
SOME HANDY HINTS FOR GOOD NOTES

Before you begin to write your notes:
1. Make sure you have **understood** what you have read.
2. Make sure what you have read is **relevant.**
3. **Think** about the most important points and how they fit together.

Once you begin to write your notes:
1. Keep your notes **brief.**
2. **Do not copy out** large pieces of text.
3. Use only **brief** and **important** quotations. Remember to use quotation marks for any quotation copied from a book. Take a note of the page number and bibliography details.

Key points in your notes can be emphasized by:
1. Capital letters
2. Underlining
3. Boxes
4. Highlighting

Your notes can be a mixture of lots of different ways of recording information

Fig. 8.6 *Guidelines for note taking for pupils of Ross High, Preston Lodge and Musselburgh Grammar school*

Figure 8.7 shows teachers' and school librarian's notes which are used in Grantown Grammar School as part of a cross-curricular project on food in Year 2 (age 13 years). The project is jointly taught by the home economics, computing and English departments and the school librarian and reinforces skills taught to pupils in Year 1 of this secondary school.

TAKING NOTES

1	**Introduction**	Importance of good note taking
		When to take notes in school
		Jobs using note taking skills

2   Exercise 1   Defining key facts in a piece of writing

Pupils read through a simple passage and have to identify the key fact(s) in each paragraph. (Passage enclosed taken from book *A taste of Italy*). Class discussion, results put up on board. Importance of understanding passage and not copying chunks or writing in sentences highlighted.

3   Exercise 2   Organizing notes

Pupils practise basic note taking using a list and a spider diagram. Advantages of each discussed. (Two passages are enclosed: 'Germany food and drink' and 'Italian ice-cream' depending on reading ability.)

Pupils take more detailed notes using preferred method from one of their own information sources. (Marked as homework.)

4   Exercise 3   Distinguishing between facts and sales talk

As so many pupils write away and obtain information from commercial organizations, it is a good opportunity to introduce this topic. Pupils are given a leaflet on German sausages and told to make notes on the introductory paragraphs, using only information which can be called 'definitely true'. Class discussion and self-assessment.

Fig. 8.7 *Note taking guidance for pupils of Grantown Grammar School*

Conclusion

Note taking can be seen as both a process which pupils go through in relation to reading, understanding and recording information and ideas and as a set of skills which can be acquired through introduction and practice. It is the process which is the most important element of note taking because if pupils understand *why* they are taking notes and what they will use the notes for, their subsequent note taking techniques will serve as a method of achieving their purpose. If pupils, on the other hand, have good note taking techniques but no real sense of purpose, then their techniques will be of little use to them when it comes to using the notes in a constructive way. The use of frames or grids to guide younger pupils into effective note taking by posing questions and, therefore, providing pupils with an in-built purpose is an excellent way of promoting good note taking habits amongst pupils. These pupils can then carry this experience further up the school where they can impose their own questions on their self-created frames. Whether pupils are using books, journals or CD-ROMs, the taking of notes from such information sources will not differ significantly, except where pupils may wish to download diagrams or photographs from the CD-ROM. The dangers of excessive copying via downloading of text and images exist in all schools now but careful guidance by teachers and school librarians and a keen sense of purpose on the part of pupils can serve to eliminate or at least to limit this practice.

Teaching Plan

A class of 24 pupils in their fourth year of secondary school are being asked to complete an assignment in computer studies. Pupils have to choose a topic relating to an aspect of information technology and society, e.g. in industry, in services such as banking, in local or central government, in the home, at school. The format, length and marking criteria of the assignment have previously been explained to the pupils. Each lesson lasts 40 minutes.

Lesson 4: Note taking

1 This class takes place in the school library. Class enter, get settled and are given a sheet (similar to Figure 8.6) on hints for note taking (5 minutes).

2 The school librarian briefly explains that the aims of the lesson are to:

   ✔ remind pupils of the PLUS model
   ✔ examine different styles of note taking amongst pupils
   ✔ discuss the importance of not copying material from books or CD-ROMs
   ✔ examine the use of key words when taking notes (5 minutes).

3 The school librarian splits the class into groups of four. Pupils are asked to give their notes on the newspaper article to another pupil in the group. Each pupil reads the other's notes and has to write down, (a) what the article is about, and (b) a possible headline for that article.

The school librarian then selects pupils to talk about how they took notes and the results of the comparisons of notes and comments on the note taking process (15 minutes).

4 Still in groups, the pupils discuss how they have used key words to take notes in the sources they have used for their computer studies assignment and the school librarian selects examples to reinforce the use of key words (10 minutes).

5 The school librarian reminds pupils that copying is plagiarism and that copied passages must not be included in assignments. Pupils are asked to draw up a presentation plan for their assignment for next week's lesson. Pupils leave (5 minutes).

References

1 Tabberer, R., *Study and information skills in schools*, NFER–Nelson, 1987.
2 Howe, M., *A teacher's guide to the psychology of learning*, Blackwell, 1984.
3 Selmes, I., *Improving study skills*, Hodder and Stoughton, 1987.
4 Wray, D. and Lewis, M., 'Extending interactions with non-fiction texts: an EXIT into understanding', *Reading*, 29 (1), April 1995, 2–9.
5 ibid.
6 Howe, M., op cit.
7 Williams, D. A. and Herring, J. E., *Keywords and learning*, RGIT, 1986.
8 Tabberer, R., op cit.
9 Claxton, G., *Teaching to learn*, Cassell, 1990.
10 BigSix listserv message 05.06.1996. The BigSix listserv was created to encourage discussion on Eisenberg and Berkovitz's BigSix model of information skills teaching and learning in schools. To subscribe, email to Listserv@listserv.syr.edu with: Subscribe BigSix Firstname Lastname (e.g. subscribe BigSix James Herring) in the text of the message.
11 Wray, D. and Lewis, M., op cit.
12 BigSix listserv, op. cit.

Chapter 9
Communication and presentation

After reading this chapter, you will be able to:

✔ **identify the links between communication and purpose for pupils doing assignments**
✔ **evaluate pupils' knowledge of audience and assessment**
✔ **identify a range of skills pupils use when writing**
✔ **evaluate methods used in oral and IT based presentations by pupils.**

In the PLUS model of information skills – purpose, location, use and self-evaluation – using information and ideas located in information resources will include communicating or presenting new knowledge, often in the form of a written or verbal presentation, to a specified audience – more often than not the subject teacher. Although a variety of forms of presentation are becoming more common in schools with the increased access pupils have to video and particularly IT based packages such as Pagemaker and Powerpoint, the written assignment remains the most common form of presentation. Teaching pupils how to communicate effectively for different purposes is seen as a general educational aim for all schools but for pupils, the most important aspects of communication in their school careers relate to those aspect of communication (e.g. written essays or reports) which are assessed by teachers. Anecdotal evidence from schools shows that pupils are often unsure how important different aspects of presentation are in the eyes of teachers. For example, some pupils (and students in higher education) put great efforts into using visual images on the front of reports or essays and including graphs, scanned images or photographs in the body of the essay or report. The main problem lies in the fact that these same pupils do not put enough effort into the written content of the report or essay and are often disappointed when they receive low marks. Thus it is important that teachers and school librarians fully explain not only what a good essay or report should contain but also how the different aspects will be assessed.

Each school will have developed guidance for pupils on communication and this chapter will attempt to provide general guidelines and examples of good practice from schools in relation to linking communication (i.e. the product of the pupil's research) and presentation (how that product is to be presented) to purpose, audience and assessment, writing skills, oral presentations and IT based presentations.

Communication and purpose

For communication, in the form of a project or assignment, to be effective, it should meet the original aims or purpose set by the pupil. The importance of purpose cannot be underestimated because the *lack* of a clear purpose will become very apparent when the pupil submits the assignment to be marked by the teacher. When teachers comment on lack of structure or organization of ideas within an assignment, they are implying that the pupil has failed to *think* through the aims of the assignment from the beginning. Thus it can be argued that some pupils' project work is doomed to achieving low marks if there is an inauspicious start to the project because the pupil does not establish a clear purpose. Teaching communication to pupils – whether written, oral or IT based –needs to emphasize thinking skills in relation to analysis, synthesis and interpretation of information and ideas located in information resources. It also needs to concentrate on evaluation (e.g. of what new knowledge pupils have gained and how that new knowledge can be incorporated into the essay or report) and repackaging (e.g. how the pupils put information and ideas into their own words or how they use quotations). It is vital, therefore, that teachers and school librarians make pupils aware of these skills *before* they teach skills of presentation.

Irving emphasizes the need for pupils to be encouraged to relate to purpose when writing assignments and argues that pupils should be taught about the importance of structuring their assignments. Irving states that 'a *sense* of structure can improve the pupil's ability to think clearly and marshal both facts and analyses' and that one way of developing this sense of structure is to encourage pupils to use their concept maps as a guide to structure.[1] This use of key words included in concept maps is reflected by Williams and Herring who argue that if pupils can follow through the sequence of identifying key words, using them to locate information resources (e.g. in the library), using key words to identify key ideas and information within these resources, using them as headings within note taking and then as subheadings within the assignment, then pupils will more easily be able to maintain the purpose of the assignment within the written and diagrammatic form of the assignment. Figure 9.1 is an example of this guidance.[2]

Lewis and Wray's research into the use of writing frames to help pupils improve their writing of assignments also stresses the need for pupils to relate their writing clearly to an established purpose and they argue that, when pupils are being introduced to ways of presenting their findings, it is very important that this is done in the context of actual topic work within a school subject and not in a separate study skills lesson. Lewis and Wray state that 'Our use of a writing frame always arose from the child having a *purpose* for undertaking some writing'.[3]

Howe argues that, 'In learning to write effectively, it is necessary to combine and co-ordinate an intimidating variety of skills'.

If pupils can be taught to realize that relating back to purpose is one of the key skills in writing, then other skills in writing cited by Howe may prove less intimidating for the pupils. Howe lists these skills as including 'handwriting, spelling, punctuation, word choice, syntax, textual connections, purpose, organisation, clarity, rhythm, euphony and reader characteristics' and states that as pupils become more experienced in writing, many of the skills are used automatically.[4]

Keyword your ideas:

- use main keywords as headings for sections or chapters or illustrations
- use keywords to label diagrams and illustrations
- use keywords to INDEX your presentation.

Fig. 9.1 *Advice on using keywords – from* Keywords and learning

Audience and assessment

In most cases in secondary schools, the audience for the pupil's presentation will be the teacher but in some subjects, pupils will be encouraged to present a report on a topic to their peers. As was noted above, it is important that teachers and school librarians recognize the difference between teaching pupils how to present information and ideas as a general skill which they may use when they leave school (e.g. when presenting reports to colleagues at work) and teaching pupils the more formalized methods of writing essays and reports which will be assessed by the teacher. For the pupils, the latter is certainly more important although the former may be more attractive. Thus if the audience is the teacher and the teacher is the assessor, it is clearly necessary for teachers to explain what they expect to read, listen to or look at when pupils' assignments are presented. Selmes urges teachers to make clear to pupils what written assignments should contain and states that teachers should stress that 'Writing is a task experienced in studying all subjects and it is generally the task which is assessed. Academic success, to a large extent, therefore, depends on skills in writing. Individual subjects have their own conventions for structuring writing... Pupils should ensure that their subject teachers make very clear what is required in their subjects'.[5]

Examples from schools

Pupils, therefore, need guidance on what is expected and the more detailed that guidance is, the more chance there is that pupils will heed the guidance given. Figure 9.2 shows advice given to pupils in Webster's High School's Country Profile project and indicates that pupils have a choice of presentation method (booklet or poster) but that the presentation should contain a number of elements (e.g. map, graph, table). Figure 9.3 shows pupils how a presentation might be structured and, by implication, demonstrates to pupils what the audience (the teacher) expects to see in a presentation on a particular country and the criteria for assessing the work.

Good Presentation methods:
Present your material under headings. Use your keywords.
Make your headings stand out from the rest of the material.
Place drawings beside the relevant facts.
Vary your drawings. Include some of the following: graphs, tables,
diagrams, cartoons, maps
All maps have a title, north point, scale and key.
Draw a frame around your map to make it stand out.

Fig. 9.2 *Recommended methods for pupils of Webster's High School*

Country Profile   (Presenting)

(Example)   Poster layout plan

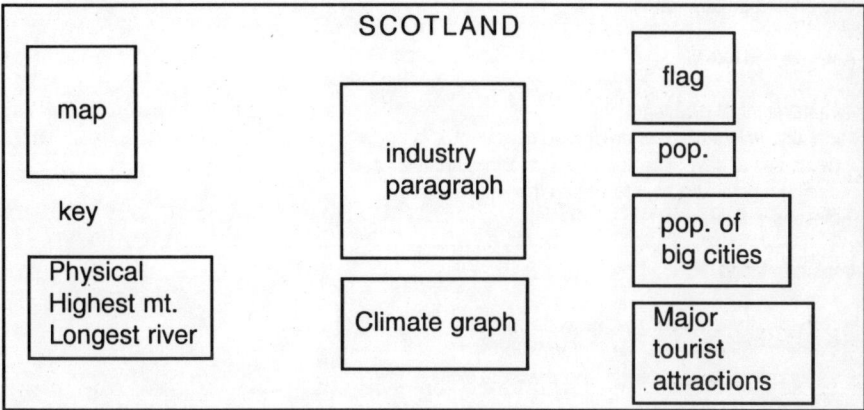

SCOTLAND

map

key

flag

industry
paragraph

pop.

pop. of
big cities

Physical
Highest mt.
Longest river

Climate graph

Major
tourist
attractions

(Example)   Booklet page layout plan

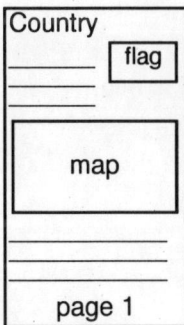

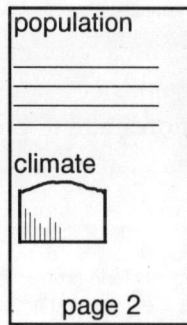

Country

flag

map

page 1

population

climate

page 2

Fig. 9.3 *Choice of presentation methods for pupils of Webster's High
School*

Figure 9.4 shows guidelines given to pupils studying for the Scottish Higher Grade Computing Studies, part of which is an investigation carried out by pupils. The assessment criteria are provided in a way which shows pupils what is expected in terms of the skills they should demonstrate but also the spread of marks which shows pupils how different skills are awarded different levels of marks. In the marks awarded for each stage in Figure 9.4, the skills of *presentation* only account for five marks out of 30 whereas skills relating to content of the assignment are much more important.

Investigation   Guidance for pupils

SIMPLIFIED ASSESSMENT CRITERIA

You should be able to:

Analysis and Design

– interpret initial problem
– identify main stages to be carried out
– decide what new information and techniques are needed
– decide where and how to obtain this information
– discuss with teacher

Implementation

– carry out the planned stages systematically (keep a log)
– extract and collate relevant information
– apply previous knowledge and practical skills
– draw valid conclusions

Evaluation

– assess to what extent the original aims have been fulfilled
– identify any limitations or possible improvement

Presentation

– prepare a report which is accurate
                              clearly stated
                              complete

Study skills

– discuss progress (and problems)
– show initiative, enthusiasm and persistence

Fig. 9.4 *Assessment criteria for Higher Grade Computing Studies Investigation*

Pupils will, therefore, benefit from clear instructions on how to present assignments to teachers in the form of essays or reports and if these clear instructions encourage pupils to think about the content of the assignment i.e. the new knowledge which is being presented, then pupils are more likely to meet the expectations of teachers when the assignments are assessed. Understanding the audience is, for pupils, a complicated skill since they will have to appreciate that different teachers in different subject areas will, to some extent, be a different audience. While the most successful pupils will learn this as if by instinct, other pupils will need firm guidance on what is expected.

Writing skills

Lewis and Wray's project identified six genres of non-fiction writing which pupils might engage in: recount, report, explanation, discussion, exposition and procedure, and their work explains how writing frames can be used with pupils in primary and early secondary schools to improve the quality of writing. Pupils often have difficulty with non-fiction writing as opposed to narrative writing, according to Lewis and Wray and, 'Some have reasons to do with the features of non-fiction texts themselves and others may stem from the model of teaching we offer our pupils'.[6]

Figure 9.5 shows Selmes's classification of different types of writing similar to that of Lewis and Wray and Selmes states that pupils can be shown versions of this table, which can be adapted for different subjects, and asked to consider how they might use the different writing qualities in their own assignments.

Embedded within these outlines are a large number of different skills which pupils will have learned at various stages of their school career but pupils will need refresher sessions to remind them not only what the various skills are but also how they should be used in different curricular contexts.

COMMON PURPOSES	WRITING QUALITIES
1. To show knowledge by describing subject perhaps to assist in later recall or revision	Record of accurate information, ideas, content, definitions or instructions
2. To summarise content or argument	Identification of the most important aspects – key points
3. To explain or show understanding	Presentation of information etc. in own words; showing the relationships between aspects; making appropriate use of vocabulary
4. To develop an argument; present evidence and draw conclusions	Selection of relevant and important points with illustrative examples; generalisation from detail; statement of implications
5. To show personal thoughts or views; to discuss; to persuade others of a point of view	As 4 above plus: inclusion of feeling, experience and an awareness of other opinion, experience and an awareness of other viewpoints

Fig. 9.5 *Types of writing identified in* Improving study skills

Structuring the presentation

Pupils will also be given advice on how to structure their writing within an assignment. Figure 9.6 shows guidance given to pupils at Grantown Grammar School and notes that pupils will be given particular guidance in different school departments.

PRESENTATION

You will receive advice on the appropriate style for your report from your department. This is some general advice.

a) Make sure that what you have written makes sense.
b) Make sure that your headings match the information you have given.
c) Make sure that the information is in a logical order – well organised.
d) Make sure you have an introduction and a conclusion.
e) Make sure you have included a title page with your name on it, a contents page and a bibliography – a list of resources you have used.

Fig. 9.6 *Presentation advice for pupils of Grantown Grammar School*

Figure 9.7 shows guidance given to pupils at Ross High, Preston Lodge and Musselburgh Grammar Schools on the importance of having a logical structure when writing assignments and Figure 9.8 shows a flow chart given to pupils in these schools.

Some advice on structuring a presentation

Arrange your notes into three main sections.
These main sections will be the three main sections of your presentation. These main sections are:

A. The Introduction
This is your chance to tell your audience what the work is about. You should cover the answers to some of the **main key questions** you asked yourself at the planning stage, such as:
  why you chose this topic
  what the topic is about
  what you wanted to find out
  how your material and information was gathered.

B. the findings or main part
This part contains all the relevant information you found out for your project. It should:
answer the **key questions** you asked yourself at the planning stage
be arranged in a logical order
contain headings and subheadings
make use of illustrations, graphs, tables etc. as appropriate.

C. The conclusion
This part should allow you to sum up the answers you found to your key questions. You should also include some thoughts and feelings of your own on the subject.

Fig. 9.7 *Structuring a presentation for pupils at Ross High, Preston Lodge and Musselburgh Grammar schools*

The above outline and examples of guidance in relation to writing skills obviously does not cover all aspects of writing in secondary schools but can be used in conjunction with aspects of writing such as sentence construction, grammar, variety of expression, use of subject terminology and appropriate use of quotations in assignments. What is clear from research in schools is that writing skills are not the responsibility of the English department alone but of all departments in the school, including the school library and it is important that all teachers and school librarians in schools pay close attention to writing skills and provide advice on such skills in the context of subject based assignment work. It should not be assumed that all pupils will have developed writing skills to the same degree nor should it be assumed that an individual pupil will have developed writing skills to the same extent in all subjects. Motivation is a key aspect of writing skills development and pupils who are more interested in particular subjects (and therefore more motivated to take advice) are more likely to develop better writing skills in those subjects than in others.

Oral presentations

An increasing number of schools across the world are encouraging pupils to use oral presentations as part of a final assignment submission. Oral presentations give pupils an opportunity to express their ideas and show the results of their research in a way which is different from traditional written assignments and in which they can explain key issues both orally and graphically. For teachers and school librarians using this form of assessment, it is important that pupils understand the criteria for awarding marks to oral presentations, that is, pupils need to understand what is being assessed, i.e. the content of their assignment, for example, an explanation of the causes of flooding in a particular area of the country *or* the skills used to provide this explanation, for example, use of voice, use of OHP, handouts, etc. *or* both of these. It was noted above that some pupils pay too much attention to the design of their assignments and too little to the actual content and the problem can arise equally with oral presentations. Because oral presentations are attractive to pupils, especially those who feel confident about speaking to an audience, they may tend to put too much emphasis on the form of the presentation as opposed to the content. When pupils are invited to give oral presentations, teachers and school librarians can emphasize the above points by showing pupils what a 'good' or 'bad' presentation looks like and can draw attention to the key issues. Pupils experience 'presentations' by teachers and school librarians almost every day but will not associate everyday teaching with being asked to give a presentation on the assignment.

There are a number of general publications on giving presentations, mostly geared towards adults but the main principles of giving oral presentations are the same for adults as for school pupils. Planning the talk is the first step which pupils will be made aware of and Rawlins uses familiar guidelines for preparing presentations, stating that presenters need to consider:

✔ the aim of the presentation (the *Why*)
✔ the content (the *What*)
✔ the audience (the *Who*)
✔ the learning method (the *How*)
✔ the learning environment (the *When* and *Where*).[7]

Pupils can be reminded that preparing presentations involves many of the same skills they used when starting their project or assignment, in particular purpose and identification of key words. A common fault of presentations by school pupils and university students is that the presenter often does not make enough use of the written content of the assignment when making the presentation. For example, a pupil making an oral presentation on computer crime as part of an overall assignment, will have structured his/her assignment using key words (e.g. hacking, computer fraud and software pirating) identified at the purpose and location stages of the project. The key word headings would seem to be the obvious subheading to use in the presentation but, in this author's experience, some pupils or students do not follow the information skills process through to the oral presentation stage. Pupils then need to be taught the importance of using their original structure in the oral presentation. Figure 9.8 shows guidance given to pupils at Cramlington Community High School on planning presentations.

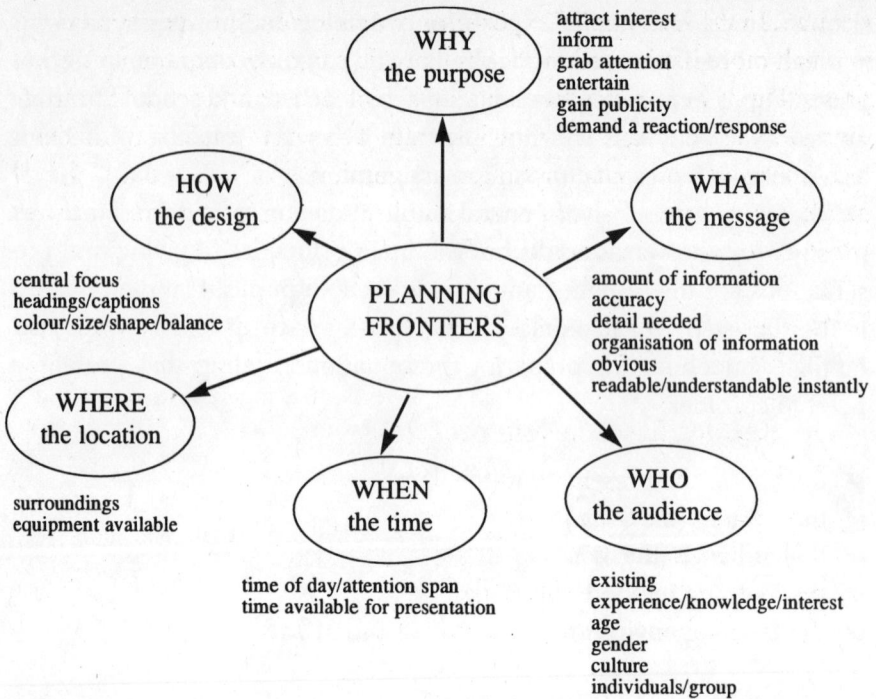

Fig. 9.8 *How to plan a presentation at Cramlington Community High School*

Pupils will also need help in selecting the use of presentation aids such as an overhead projector (OHP). Even if pupils are accustomed to teachers and school librarians using OHPs in the classroom or library, it should not be assumed that the pupils will have any understanding of how to use an OHP effectively. Pupils should be given trial runs to identify common faults such as obscuring the screen or not checking to see whether all the acetate can be seen or not switching off the OHP during the presentation. Other aids such as flip charts, diagrams or charts or slides all present individual problems which, with practice, can be overcome.

The key to oral presentations, given suitably structured and intellectually coherent content, is delivery. The ability of pupils to deliver oral presentations will very much depend on what experience they have had in making presentations in their school career. In some countries such as the USA, high school pupils/students take speech communication classes as part of their curriculum and are taught presentational skills within the curriculum. In the UK, pupils' experience of making oral presentations tends to much more haphazard, with many pupils having no experience of oral presentations before the third or fourth year of secondary school. Pupils then need to be taught the principles and techniques of delivery, including aspects of body language: how to stand, use of eye contact, use of hands, etc. Figure 9.9 shows Mandel's illustrative guide on what to avoid when giving an oral presentation.[8]

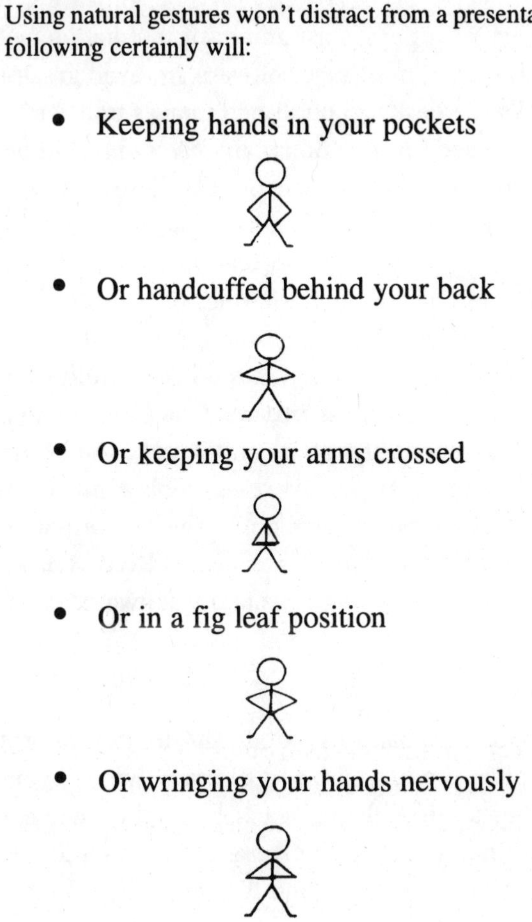

Using natural gestures won't distract from a presentation; however, doing one of the following certainly will:

- Keeping hands in your pockets

- Or handcuffed behind your back

- Or keeping your arms crossed

- Or in a fig leaf position

- Or wringing your hands nervously

Fig. 9.9 *Advice on using body language, from* Effective presentation skills

Pupils can be reminded of the need to structure their delivery as they did their assignment in that they should provide an introduction, the key content and a conclusion in the oral presentation.

IT based presentations

As pupils become increasingly sophisticated at using IT and as schools acquire more hardware and software to be used by pupils, the use of pre-sentational software such as Powerpoint is likely to become fairly common in schools in the next few years. The simplicity of use of this type of software means that pupils can deliver presentations which include a range of presentational techniques including the use of sound, video, photography as well as clip art images. Using Powerpoint-type software can certainly enhance the delivery of a pupil's assignment presentation but the dangers of the superficial attraction of such software are even greater than those found when pupils use desk top published images transferred on to OHPs. The fact that IT based presentations can *appear* to be almost as sophisticated as some graphical images seen on TV can often lead pupils to seek to perfect the medium while ignoring the message, i.e. emphasizing presentation over content. Pupils therefore need to be reminded that using IT does not change the basic rules of planning, use of argument and presentation of research findings and coherent structure within a presentation. Powerpoint's introduction in the User's Guide will tell pupils that, 'Powerpoint has it all. Prompts, tips and Cue Cards to help you learn the product quickly; wizards, templates and AutoLayouts help you get right to work; and a complete set of easy-to-use tools assures you have everything you need to get your point across and share information with others',[9] but pupils will need more guidance on using IT based products for presentations than what appears in guides to the software.

Conclusion

Communication of information and ideas by pupils, mostly in the form of assessed assignments, is often the final product of many weeks' work by the pupils. This communication with the teacher or other assessor shows the pupil's ability to understand the purpose of the assignment, locate relevant information resources, understand the concepts and ideas within these sources, select relevant material and write a coherent essay or report which reflects the key issues of the topic and may contain some of the pupil's own views. Effective communication therefore means that the pupil has to master and demonstrate a wide range of interrelated cognitive and affective skills in order to gain the esteem of the teacher and high marks. The need for teachers and school librarians to involve the pupils in the *processes* of communication – whether it be written, oral or IT based – cannot be underestimated if pupils are to understand not only how to communicate in different ways but also *why* they are asked to do so. Pupils who are given explanations of the teacher or school librarian's experience of communication in different forms and who are allowed to practise these skills within curricular contexts are more likely to meet the standards set by the school.

Teaching Plan

A class of 24 pupils in their fourth year of secondary school are being asked to complete an assignment in computer studies. Pupils have to choose a topic relating to an aspect of information technology and society, e.g. in industry, in services such as banking, in local or central government, in the home, at school. The format, length and marking criteria of the assignment have previously been explained to the pupils. Each lesson lasts for 40 minutes.

Lesson 5: Presentation

1 Class enter, get settled and are given a sheet on structuring a presentation (similar to Figure 9.7). They are asked to take out their assignment presentation plans (5 minutes).
2 The teacher briefly explains that the aims of the lesson are:

   ✔ to remind pupils of the PLUS model
   ✔ to examine aspects of written presentations
   ✔ to highlight the use of keywords in writing assignments
   ✔ to give pupils practice in planning an oral presentation
      (5 minutes).

3 The teacher takes the pupils through the sheet on structure, highlighting the key points. Pupils are then asked to discuss their assignment plan with another pupil and to suggest improvements or amendments in each other's plan, especially in relation to the use of keywords (10 minutes).
4 The teacher chooses one pupil's plan in each group and asks the group to prepare a plan for an oral presentation in which each group can use

two OHPs. Pupils write down the headings on paper with brief notes attached. The teacher selects examples and comments on the plans, explaining the differences between oral and written presentations (15 minutes).

5 The teacher sums up what has been learned and gives pupils a self-evaluation questionnaire to fill in for next week's lesson. Pupils leave (5 minutes).

References

1 Irving, A., *Study and information skills across the curriculum*, Heinemann, 1987.
2 Williams, D. A. and Herring, J. E., *Keywords and learning*, RGIT, 1986.
3 Lewis, M. and Wray, D., *Writing frames: scaffolding children's non-fiction writing in a range of genres*, Exeter University, 1996.
4 Howe, M., *A teacher's guide to the psychology of learning*, Blackwell, 1984.
5 Selmes, I., *Improving study skills*, Hodder and Stoughton, 1987.
6 Lewis, M. and Wray, D., op cit.
7 Rawlins, K., *Presentation and communication skills*, Macmillan Magazines, 1993.
8 Mandel, S., *Effective presentation skills*, Kogan Page, 1987.
9 *Microsoft Powerpoint user's guide*, Microsoft, 1994.

Chapter 10
Self-evaluation

After reading this chapter, you will be able to:

✔ **understand aspects of reflective and experiential learning theory**
✔ **assess how pupils examine their assignment work**
✔ **evaluate methods of teaching pupils self-evaluation**
✔ **recognize the constraints faced by staff in schools in teaching self-evaluation skills to pupils.**

Of all the categories of information skills examined in this book – purpose, location, use and self-evaluation – the latter is perhaps the one which practitioners, such as teachers and school librarians, view as being most difficult to implement in any depth. When pupils receive written comments on assignments, teachers will urge them to examine these comments and try to learn from mistakes or omissions but often the process of encouraging self-evaluation amongst pupils goes no further than passing advice. Despite this, teachers and school librarians recognize the importance of self-evaluation amongst pupils because they have evidence that those pupils who do reflect on their own learning and performance in coursework can make dramatic improvements, for example in the use of subject based terminology or the structuring of assignments. More systematic methods are thus needed to build self-evaluation into the learning process so that pupils themselves recognize that this is an integral part of their school work as well as being a means by which to improve their own performance.

This chapter will examine the theories of reflective and experiential learning, how pupils can evaluate their assignment work, how pupils can evaluate their overall learning performance and the constraints faced by teachers and school librarians in teaching self-evaluation to pupils in secondary schools.

Reflective and experiential learning

Kolb's theories

As was seen in Chapter 1, pupils bring a variety of experiences of learning to each new learning situation, whether that be learning new concepts or techniques in class following instruction from the teacher or seeking relevant sources of information about these concepts in the school library in order to take notes to form the basis of an assignment around these concepts. The ability of pupils to reflect on past experience, in the form of transferring skills or ensuring that mistakes or omissions are not repeated, is crucial to the learning process. The work of Kolb has been cited by a number of authors to stress the importance of reflective and experiential learning amongst pupils. Kolb's four modes of learning include:

✔ concrete experience, emphasizes how pupils feel about their learning in relation to new ideas and working with others
✔ reflective observation, emphasizes how pupils examine new ideas and concepts by detailed observation as opposed to actual experience and how pupils can study these concepts and ideas from different perspectives
✔ abstract conceptualization, emphasizes how pupils think logically about new concepts or ideas and how they might apply scientific methods of evaluating particular theories
✔ active experimentation, emphasizes how pupils learn from doing and using practical applications in their learning situations.[1]

Pupils will use all of Kolb's categories at some point during their time at school and some pupils will prefer some methods over others. In relation to information skills, Kolb's modes of learning highlight the importance of different approaches needed by pupils involved in assignment work and some elements, such as reflective observation can be used at different stages of an assignment. Thus pupils can reflect on:

✔ what they already know when identifying purpose
✔ what sources they might use when locating information and ideas

✔ the relevance or suitability of information resources when they are using books, journals, CD-ROMs or the Internet
✔ what they have written in their assignment at the communication stage
✔ their overall performance at the self-evaluation stage.

The deliberate learning route

Whitaker argues that pupils can be encouraged to think about learning experiences, such as completing a project or assignment, and that this can lead to them 'either sustaining or modifying . . . [their] behaviour in the light of [their] realisations'.[2]

Whitaker's deliberate learning route can be seen clearly in relation to project work in Figure 10.1. Pupils are encouraged to reflect on their completed assignment and draw conclusions both by themselves and in relation to the teacher's comments. The conclusions which pupils might come to will emerge from a study of their successful (or otherwise) implementation of information skills, such the need to have a clearer pur-

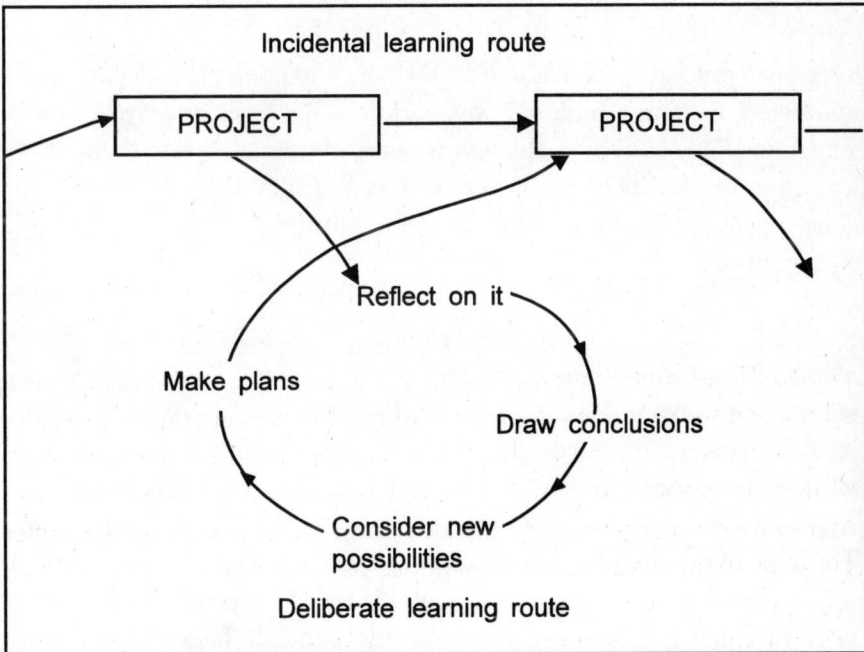

Fig. 10.1 *The deliberate learning route, from* Managing to learn

pose or to seek out more sources or to use more terminology when writing. The conclusions reached can then be used at the planning stages of the next project after examining what new (or better applied) methods might be used.

Tabberer's project raised a number of questions which are still relevant for today's schools ten years later. Tabberer asked, 'To what extent do pupils look back over their work? How do they use what they have done or the experience of how they have done it? Do pupils reflect on work completed? Do they finally evaluate their progress?'.[3]

Irving stresses that, in order for pupils to properly evaluate their own performance in marked assignments, it must be clear to pupils what is being assessed, so that they can reflect on this. Irving argues that pupils should be encouraged to identify possible improvements in their work and that, 'Discussion with peers is unquestionably valuable in forming strategies for future action'.[4]

Evaluating assignment work

Pupils can be taught how to evaluate their own work before handing it in to the teacher. In some cases, this will take the form of a more or less mechanical check to see whether the 'rules" of assignment presentation have been followed, e.g. is there a title page and contents page, are pages numbered, is there a bibliography, and does the bibliography follow set guidelines. This kind of evaluation is of a surface nature and if pupils are to undertake a deeper approach to evaluation of their project work, then questions of the kind posed by Eisenberg and Berkowitz can be suggested to pupils, including:

✔ Was the information problem solved?
✔ Was the information need met?
✔ Was the decision made?
✔ Was the situation resolved?
✔ Does the product satisfy the requirements as originally defined?[5]

This type of question is more suitable as it clearly relates to the *purpose* as opposed to the *form* of the assignment. Figure 10.2 shows guidance given to pupils doing an investigation for the Scottish Higher Computing Studies and combines questions relating to both content and form.

Check the almost finished report

- Are there any glaring spelling or grammatical mistakes?
- Is it an accurate account of your investigation?
- Have you omitted something important that you spent a lot of time doing?
- Have you acknowledged any 'extra' help you may have had?

Fig. 10.2 *Checklist for the Higher Grade Computing Studies Investigation*

Figure 10.3 shows advice given to pupils at Ross High, Preston Lodge and Musselburgh Grammar schools and is a checklist which pupils might follow when submitting an assignment. This checklist, although mainly relating to form reinforces the relation to purpose both at the beginning and in question 1.

Evaluating
Before you hand in the project

If you have used your planning sheet properly and followed the advice given, then you should have no problems with your project.

As a final check before you hand in your project, you should go through this checklist. You should be able to answer **'yes'** to every question!

Checklist

1. Have I done exactly as the assignment asked me to?
2. Are my ideas arranged in logical order?
3. Does my project have an introduction?
4. Does my project have a main part?
5. Does my project have a conclusion?
6. Does my project have an attractive cover, title page or heading?
7. Have I added a bibliography?
8. Is my work neatly set out using headings and sub-headings?
9. Is my handwriting neat?
10. Is my spelling correct?
11. Have I used more than one source of information?
12. Is my information relevant?
13. Have I used my own words?
14. Have I used inverted commas for quotations?
15. Have I included relevant illustrations and diagrams?

Fig. 10.3 *Guidance on evaluation for pupils of Ross High, Preston Lodge and Musselburgh Grammar schools*

Figure 10.4 shows Oakham School's advice to sixth form pupils on 'Learning and information skills' and includes a section on the need for pupils to evaluate their work in relation to purpose, sources of information, structure and presentation.

Evaluation skills
- Have I accomplished all I need to do?
- Have I used all relevant resources?
- Have I completed my work in the time frame?
- Have I organised and presented my work in the most helpful and appropriate manner?

Fig. 10.4 *Questions for sixth form pupils of Oakham School*

Figure 10.5 is an extract from the teachers' notes on the Country Profile project at Webster's High School. This represents a good example of Whitaker's deliberate learning route in that there is a link established between the present project and future projects in the school. It also emphasizes the difference between content and format but usefully requires pupils to evaluate the quality of presentation, which is more important in a geography project of this nature than might be the case with other projects.

EVALUATING (Review) – Reflecting on what was learned.
- Recognise strengths and weaknesses.
- Pupils are asked how their profile could have been improved.
- Both strengths and weaknesses will be developed in future assignments.
- Pupils are asked to review a variety of profiles highlighting the outstanding and weak features.
- Pupils could evaluate the profiles in terms of:

Content
- Is it just copied from books?
- Are there any original ideas?
- Is it accurate?
- Is the layout logical?

Presentation
- Are the illustrations well presented?
- Is there a bibliography?
- What are its outstanding features?
- What are its weak features?

Fig. 10.5 *Teachers' notes on self-evaluation from Webster's High School*

By asking pupils to evaluate their own assignments, teachers and school librarians are encouraging the pupils to take an active part in examining their own information skills and if this kind of evaluation can be built into project work across the curriculum, then pupils will come to accept it as a natural part of doing an assignment, no matter what subject is involved. This would then increase the possibility of pupils transferring the skills learned in one project to the next project they work on.

Evaluating performance

Involving pupils in the learning process is a difficult task for teachers and school librarians as pupils often take the view that the *process* is something which teachers are concerned with, in that they teach pupils how to take an effective part in that process. Pupils, therefore, tend to see themselves as active participants in the learning process but not as people who actively reflect on that process. Asking pupils to evaluate their performance in relation to assignment work in which they have put information skills into action is a complicated issue because of the wide number of factors involved. A pupil's 'performance' will be judged by the written, verbal or IT based presentation which the pupil makes but the reflection on this performance will include aspects such as motivation, organization of time and amount of time spent on the assignment as well as the pupil's identification of purpose, location of information resources and effective use of resources in terms of note taking and writing. In Chapter 1, the variety of aspects which affect learning were identified and these aspects need to be considered when asking pupils to evaluate performance. The pupil's performance in completing assignments should not be isolated from his/her overall performance in school, e.g. in terms of commitment, relationships with staff and peers, how 'hard' the pupil works or how willing the pupil is to participate in classroom discussions.

A number of these issues are tackled by study skills guides but most of these guides are written either for the 'ideal' pupil or in a way which is so impersonal that individual pupils find it hard to relate to them. Some schools, such as Oakham School, produce guides for pupils which encourage them to reflect on their role as a pupil in school. Such guides are useful if they allow individual pupils the opportunity to relate what is said in the guides to their own personal situation. Figure 10.6 is an extract from Oakham School's booklet for general studies 'Optimizing your performance' and asks pupils to reflect on their attitudes towards their work in school. This extract forms part of a series of issues highlighted for pupils and the booklet includes advice on the myths of the super student, organizing time, using the library, reading skills, note taking, dealing with anxiety and revision.

Figure 10.7 is an exercise given to pupils at Ross High, Preston Lodge and Musselburgh Grammar schools and follows on from Figure 10.3

DISCOVER YOUR ATTITUDE TOWARDS STUDYING

		Yes	No
1.	I am satisfied with my scores in tests and exams.	☐	☐
2.	If I do poorly in a test, I increase my efforts and get help from a teacher, or fellow pupil.	☐	☐
3.	When required, I can concentrate on studying, I am not easily distracted.	☐	☐
4.	The challenge of making notes on a difficult textbook reading does not throw me.	☐	☐
5.	Although I am busy I can still find priority time to study. Procrastination and cramming are not problems for me.	☐	☐
6.	I pay attention in class and carefully prepare ahead for most classes.	☐	☐
7.	I have a clear reason for going to school.	☐	☐
8.	When I have a boring teacher, I realise I must work harder to make the material interesting.	☐	☐
9.	My moods or personal problems seldom prevent me from completing my work.	☐	☐
10.	I can visualise myself passing the exams.	☐	☐
11.	I know how to reward myself for finishing a difficult prep.	☐	☐
12.	I listen carefully while taking class notes, and I revise them within 24 hours.	☐	☐

Fig. 10.6 *Extract from Oakham School's* Optimising your performance *booklet*

Reflection
On the process you went through

1. Briefly outline the steps you went through in your project. Your planning sheet will help you.
2. List the resources you used. Are there any you wish now that you had used?
3. Did you have any problems with the project? If so-
   What were the problems?
   How did you solve them?
4. Did you **enjoy** doing the project?
5. Did you **learn** anything new or interesting by doing the project?
6. What new skills did you learn?
7. Did you discover anything you now wish to improve on?

Fig. 10.7 Reflection on performance from Ross High, Preston Lodge and Musselburgh Grammar schools' Information and Study Skills booklet

above. This exercise is followed up by discussion of the results by the pupils themselves so that they can not only reflect on their own performance but can also learn from others also.

Reflection is, therefore, a very important part of self-evaluation for pupils but for reflection to be deliberate and not accidental, teachers and school librarians need to ensure that reflection is integrated into assignment work, so that pupils become accustomed to looking back on their work and the processes involved in that work and consciously attempting to learn from their own strengths and weaknesses in different areas of the curriculum.

Constraints

There a number of difficulties faced by teachers and school librarians in teaching pupils how to evaluate their performance in relation to specific assignments and in relation to their overall performance in school.

The first difficulty is that the individual learning styles of pupils will differ in some respects and it will not be easy for staff to draw up self-evaluation schedules which will meet the needs of individual pupils. The use of study skills questionnaires covering attitudes to school work, to different subjects areas, to homework can be useful for most pupils but some individual pupils may find that such questionnaires do not fit their own style.

The second difficulty in relation to self-evaluation lies in convincing pupils, especially younger, less mature pupils of the value of self-evaluation. As was noted above, many pupils regard evaluation as being the job of the teacher or school librarian and may take the view that it is the person who teaches them who should evaluate the performance and then instruct the pupils on how they should improve their performance. Unfortunately, as was seen in Chapter 1, learning is a complicated process which *requires* input from the learner if improvement in the form of transferability of skills is to occur.

The third constraint lies in the fact that often there is little time in the curriculum for reflection, in that pupils have no sooner finished one project than they are on to another or that when pupils complete one assignment, their full attention is immediately switched to an assignment in another subject area. Given this scenario, it is difficult for teachers and librarians to motivate pupils to take time to reflect on their performance when the school system is pushing them in another direction.

The final constraint also relates to time but in this case it is the time needed by teachers and school librarians to talk to pupils about the evaluations which the pupils carry out, for example, in the form of questionnaires issued by guidance teachers or specific forms to be filled in at the end of particular assignments. Given that secondary school classes in the UK can contain up to 30 pupils, the time which the teacher would need to discuss the pupils' individual performances simply does not exist.

Conclusion

Self-evaluation is the final step in the information skills process of purpose, location, use and self-evaluation but it is also the starting point for future work done by pupils. Self-evaluation requires pupils to be honest with themselves and to take a mature attitude to their school work and this can cause problems with some pupils who may lack the maturity to recognize the importance of self-evaluation within the learning process. To overcome some of the constraints noted above, teachers and school librarians can help pupils to recognize the importance of self-evaluation both by integrating aspects of evaluation into assignment specifications and by encouraging pupils to discuss evaluation amongst themselves.

Teaching Plan

A class of 24 pupils in their fourth year of secondary school are being asked to complete an assignment in computer studies. Pupils have to choose a topic relating to an aspect of information technology and society, e.g. in industry, in services such as banking, in local or central government, in the home, at school. The format, length and marking criteria of the assignment have previously been explained to the pupils. Each lesson lasts 40 minutes.

Lesson 6: Self-evaluation

1 This lesson takes place in the school library. Class enter, get settled and hand in their self-evaluation questionnaires (5 minutes).
2 The school librarian briefly explains that the aims of the lesson are to:

   ✔ remind pupils of the PLUS model
   ✔ allow pupils to discuss why self-evaluation is important
   ✔ allow pupils to identify improvements in their assignment work in the future
   ✔ ask pupils to think about their overall performance in school (5 minutes).

3 Pupils are asked to write down three reasons why they should evaluate the assignment they have just completed. They then discuss these reasons in groups of 4 and the school librarian selects and comments positively on some of the reasons. The pupils are then given a guide to evaluating their overall performance in school (15 minutes).
4 Pupils read the evaluation advice and discuss this in groups of four and each group is asked to rank the importance of aspects such as motivation, organization of time, working 'hard' and seeking information resources outside school. The school librarian then writes selective rankings on the OHP and comments on them, asking pupils to respond (10 minutes).

5   Pupils are reminded of why self-evaluation is useful to them in their school career as well as when they leave school. Pupils leave (5 minutes).

References

1   Kolb, D., *Experiential learning*, Prentice-Hall, 1984.
2   Whitaker, D., *Managing to learn*, Cassell, 1995.
3   Tabberer, R., *Study and information skills in schools*, NFER–Nelson, 1987.
4   Irving, A., *Study and information skills across the curriculum*, Heinemann, 1985.
5   Eisenberg, M. and Berkovitz, R., *Information problem solving: the Big Six approach to library and information skills instruction*, Ablex, 1990. (Website: http://www.edweb.sdsu.edu.edfirst/bigsix/basics.html)

Chapter 11
Future developments

After reading this chapter, you will be able to:

✔ **evaluate future trends in the school curriculum**
✔ **evaluate future trends in hardware and software developments in schools**
✔ **critically examine the future development of the Internet for schools**
✔ **evaluate the implications of the above developments for information skills in schools.**

Trying to forecast what schools will be like in the medium or distant future is not an exact science, given the rapid developments in information technology and communications in the developed countries in the past ten years. In looking at schools, however, the temptation only to examine IT developments should be resisted. Schools exist for particular social, economic and political reasons which are not likely to change in the near future because of developments in, for example, multimedia communications technologies. The *purposes* of secondary schools are to to educate future citizens, provide a skilled workforce, socialize individuals into the mores of a particular society and teach a range of basic skills and they will not change dramatically, nor will they be greatly influenced by information technology. Thus, schools may teach history, for example, in a different way in the future by giving pupils online access to multimedia versions of historical documents but the *reasons* for teaching history are unlikely to change. The need for information skills in schools will definitely increase in the future because of the greatly expanded quantity of information resources which will be available to schools through IT developments. This chapter will briefly examine future trends in the school curriculum, developments in IT hardware and software, the Internet of the future and the implications of these developments for information skills teaching in schools.

The future curriculum

The topics studied in the secondary school of the future are likely to be much the same as they are today and structured in subjects such as English, Maths, Science, History, Geography etc. but there are likely to be changes in the curriculum which link subjects closer together. Treadaway suggests that 'the curriculum could be structured into: Processes (e.g. Scientific Investigation; Using and Applying Mathematics. Designing and Evaluating); subject-specific skills; and content related material (which could be grouped by subject or into different content/topic groups)'.[1]

This could mean that teachers will be expected to teach 'subjects' which cross traditional boundaries and that school librarians will be expected to support these new 'subjects' by purchasing cross-curricular books and journals as well as purchasing access to electronic information resources which can be used by pupils. Despite these changes, the skills which pupils learn in relation to literacy, numeracy and socialization are likely to remain at the forefront of a future curriculum. Within that curriculum, however, there will be more emphasis on the development of cognitive skills in problem solving, evaluation of ethical issues in relation to scientific developments and thinking skills in relation to evaluation of ideas and information located in information resources within and outside the school.

Hardware and software

The dramatic developments in digitization in IT hardware, in communications technologies and in the reduction in the cost of IT which have happened in recent years will certainly continue, giving schools much more access to up to date equipment and much improved links with external resources. The amount of money which individual schools have to spend on hardware and software will still depend on government policy and parental contribution and the existence of 'information rich' and 'information poor' schools is likely to be highlighted in the future. The reasons for differences in school budgets are likely to remain the same in the future in that fee paying schools and comprehensive schools in affluent areas will still be able to afford better technology than their less fortunate neighbours but the reduction in costs may well see some levelling in the access which different schools have to hardware.

The convergence of different technologies has been seen in schools in recent years with the advent of fax machines, multimedia PCs and the Internet and this trend will continue with schools having access to smaller but much more powerful items of IT in the future. Keegan states that the new Nokia 9000 Communicator, which is a hand-held computer which can store information, send e-mail and faxes and access the Internet is 'the marriage of the computer, the telephone and the Internet into the first pocket sized, user friendly device for around £1000. Twenty five years ago, the computing power of this machine would have cost millions of pounds and needed the space of a small village to accommodate it'.[2]

Given such developments, future schools will have at their disposal equipment which is infinitely more sophisticated (technically) than what is available now. However, the *quantity* and technical sophistication of IT equipment in schools will not necessarily produce improvements in the *quality* of pupils' learning unless the equipment is seen to support a curriculum which provides opportunities for pupils to learn more effectively.

In terms of software, the introduction of voice activated PCs will be an advantage especially to physically disadvantaged pupils and the production of packaged lessons available via the Internet will help pupils and teachers in schools if they can incorporate elements of meeting the needs of individual pupils in relation to their individual learning styles. At present, however, teaching packages tend to cater for groups of pupils or for some 'ideal' pupil. There is no doubt that what is now seen as word-processing software such as Word for Windows, will develop into software which contains elements of word processing, spreadsheet, desktop publishing and multimedia software. Thus pupils will be able to use this software to make very sophisticated presentations but as seen in Chapter 9, it is the content of a presentation which is most important in terms of the understanding the pupils show of ideas and concepts and not the presentational techniques used.

The Internet

At present, the majority of schools in developed countries do not have access to the Internet but this situation is likely to change within the next two years due to developments in communications and the desire of governments to encourage commercial companies, such as British Telecom and cable television companies, to provide links to all schools via metropolitan area networks which now cover much of the UK. The Internet is still growing and presents schools with an opportunity to access a vast range of information from across the world which can be used in all subjects in the school. The Internet is an undoubted boon for school librarians who can almost instantly increase access to information resources to a huge extent. In the near future many schools are likely to exploit information from the Internet by creating topic based CD-ROMs which contain information downloaded from Internet sites (with copyright clearance) and can be geared towards the needs of an individual school's curriculum. A pilot scheme of this kind is planned to take place at Linlithgow Academy in Scotland. Pupils will access the CD-ROMs using Netscape software loaded on to Macintosh workstations in the school library. The CD-ROMs will also be networked around the school in the near future. The problems of accessing relevant information were highlighted by the NCET's 'Libraries of the future' project and one of the reasons for the problems which pupils faced was the lack of specificity available via existing search engines such as Yahoo. McElvogue argues that new search engines being developed now will enable users to be much more specific about their individual needs when searching for information on the Internet and cites new search engines such as Pointcast, Firefly and infoSage as promising better access for users.[3]

Internet developments are likely to increase the access which schools have to online, multimedia information such as news events as well as multimedia guides to institutions such as museums and art galleries. The problems faced by teachers and school librarians in relation to pupils using the Internet are likely to remain. Thus just as educationally relevant multimedia tours of the world's art galleries will be invaluable to art teachers, the same sophistication in multimedia will be used by those propagating pornography on the Internet. Also, the existence of sexist, racist and politically subversive material on the Internet will not disappear and schools will still have to ensure that Acceptable Use Policies are constantly monitored.

Implications for information skills

In a recent article, Tony Blair, leader of the UK's Labour Party, stated that, 'In the future, an important aspect of literacy will be the ability to find, manipulate and add value to information using electronic means' and Blair argues that as technology becomes more sophisticated then the importance of being able to use information effectively will be a vital future skill.[4] Treadaway argues that future skills should be grouped around the term 'information capability' which would incorporate the range of information skills covered in this book as well as all the necessary IT skills which pupils will acquire in the future and he argues that, 'What is vital, however, is that we seriously debate the likely impact of access to massive information sources – many of which are visual or aural rather than just textual- on pupils' learning . . . Might one small step in the right direction be to get language, art and IT subject coordinators and school librarians to talk together about these issues?'[5]

The need for information skills is increasing both at school, at home and in employment and will continue to increase in the future. The PLUS model suggested in this book provides a framework which teachers and school librarians can use to increase pupils' awareness of the importance of thinking about what they read, view or listen to. The availability of information in the future will be much greater than today and this will be matched by a greater need for the effective *use* of information and ideas – in Wray and Lewis's terms, a greater interaction with texts of all kinds in order to increase understanding and learning in schools.

Conclusion

The convergence of technologies in the future needs to be accompanied by a convergence of cognitive skills in the minds of pupils if they are to be effective learners in tomorrow's schools. The roles of teachers and school librarians as educational facilitators and providers of access to electronic information sources may well merge in future schools but one of their roles will be to ensure that the range of skills brought together here under the term 'information skills' is taught to pupils across the curriculum and is reinforced in all years of secondary school. Better links with primary schools, better cooperation between teachers, school librarians and senior management in schools and improved in-service training for all school staff will be needed if the technology available in tomorrow's schools is to have a real, and not a cosmetic effect on pupils' learning.

References

1   Treadaway, M: 'Information capability 2000? A peek into the future', *School library 2000*, Issue 10, March 1996, 1, 20.
2   Keegan, V., 'The everything machine', *Online Guardian*, 01.08.96, 3.
3   McElvogue, L., 'The Web gains that personal touch', *Online Guardian*, 18.07.96, 2–3.
4   Blair, T., 'Computers and children: partnerships for the future', *Computer bulletin supplement*, April 1996.
5   Treadaway, M., op cit.

Bibliography

Atkinson, J, and Scott, N., 'Rethinking information skills teaching', *Learning resources journal*, **11** (2), June 1995, 45–8.

Australian School Library Association, *Teaching information skills*, (CD-ROM), Forthcoming.

Bell, S and Solity, J., *Classroom management, principles and practice*, Croom Helm, 1989.

Blair, Rt, Hon. T., 'Computers and children, partnerships for the future', *Computer bulletin supplement*, April 1996.

Brown, J., 'Developing information skills', in Kinnell, M., *Managing library resources in schools*, Library Association Publishing, 1994.

Carson, S. R., 'A supported self study approach to Earth in Space at Key Stage 3', *Physics education*, **30** (2), March 1995, 95–100.

Claxton, G., *Teaching to learn*, Cassell, 1990.

Cullingford, G., *Children, teachers and learning*, Cassell, 1990.

Department for Education., *English for ages 5–16*, Department for Education, 1993.

Eisenberg, M and Berkowitz, R., *Information problem solving, the big six approach to library and information skills instruction*, Ablex, 1990, (Website: http://edweb.sdsu.edu/edfirst/bigsix/basics.html)

Eisenberg, M and Berkowitz, R., 'The six habits of highly effective students', *School library journal*, August, 1995, 22–5.

Entwistle, N., *Understanding classroom learning*, Hodder and Stoughton, 1987.

Herring, J. E., (ed)., *Information technology in schools*, Library Association, 1992.

Hohn, R., *Classroom learning and teaching*, Longman USA, 1995.

Honey, P. and Mumford, A., *Manual of learning styles*, P Honey, 1986.

Howe, M., *A teacher's guide to the psychology of learning*, Blackwell, 1984.

Irving, A., *Study and information skills across the curriculum*, Heinemann, 1985.

Johnson, D., 'Student access to the Internet', *Emergency librarian*, 22 (3), Jan–Feb 1995, 8–12.

Keegan, V., 'The everything machine', *Online Guardian*, 01.08.96, 3.

Kolb, D., *Experiential learning*, Prentice Hall, 1984.

Kyriacou, C., *Essential teaching skills*, Blackwell, 1991.

LM_NET. To subscribe, e-mail to Listserve@Listserv.syr.edu and include in the message subscribe First name Last name, e.g. Subscribe James Herring.

Lewis, M and Wray, D., *Writing frames, scaffolding children's non-fiction writing in a range of genres*, Exeter University, 1996.

McElvogue, L., 'The Web gains that personal touch', *Online Guardian*, 18.07.96, 2–3.

Mackenzie, J. and Davies, H., *Filling the toolbox: classroom strategies to engender student questioning.*
http://www.pacificrim.net/~mckenzie/toolbox/html#Beginning

Mandel, S., *Effective presentation skills*, Kogan Page, 1987.

Marland, M., *The craft of the classroom*, 2nd edn, Heinemann, 1993.

Marland, M (ed)., *Information skills in the secondary curriculum*, Methuen, 1981.

Martin, F and Swift, D., 'What can CD-ROMs do for us?', *Teaching geography*, 21 (1), January 1996, 20–3.

Martin, F and Bailey, P., 'Evaluating and using resources', in *The geography teacher's handbook*, Geography Teacher's Association, 1995.

Microsoft Powerpoint User's guide, Microsoft, 1994.

Millard, E., *Developing readers in the middle years*, Open University Press, 1994.

Morrison, M and Markless, S., *Enhancing information skills in further education*, British Library, 1992.

National Council for Educational Technology, *Information skills in action*, NCET, 1993.

Rawlins, K., *Presentation and communication skills*, Macmillan Magazines, 1993.

Rogers, R (ed.), *Teaching information skills*, Bowker Saur/ British Library, 1994.

School Curriculum and Assessment Authority, *Consultation on the National Curriculum*, SCAA, 1994.

School library 2000, Issue 11, May 1996, 22–5.

Selmes, I., *Improving study skills*, Hodder and Stoughton, 1987.

Smith, C and Laslett, R., *Effective classroom management*, 2nd edn, Routledge, 1993.

Tabberer, R., *Study and information skills in schools*, NFER–Nelson, 1987.

Treadaway, M., Information capability 2000, *School library 2000*, Issue 10, March 1996, 1,20.

Turner, P., *Helping teachers teach*, Libraries Unlimited, 1993.

Wheldall, K and Glynn, T., *Effective classroom learning*, Blackwell, 1989.

Whitaker, P., *Managing to learn*, Cassell, 1995.

Williams, D. A. and Herring, J. E., *Keywords and learning*, RGIT, 1986.

Wragg, E., *Classroom teaching skills*, Routledge, 1984.

Wray, D., *Teaching information skills through project work*, Hodder and Stoughton, 1987.

Wray, D and Lewis, M., 'Extending interactions with non-fiction texts: an EXIT to understanding', *Reading*, 29 (1), April 1995, 2–9.

Index

key words 60, 66, 75–9, 89, 92, 106,
113, 116–7, 126, 136, 139, 147

learning 1–14
behaviourist theories 4–5
complexity of 5–6
experiential 154–6
reflective 154–6
strategies 9–12, 111
styles 7–9, 39, 80, 161, 167
theories 3–7
'Libraries of the future' project 26–7,
102
LM_NET 32
location 18, 39, 87–107

motivation 11, 44, 146

note taking 18, 24, 36, 70, 75, 122–36,
160
frames 128–30
and learning 124
and purpose 125–7
techniques 128–34
trash and treasure 127–8

online information 18, 25, 40
OPACs 40, 75, 76, 89, 92, 94, 95, 99,
106

planning
lessons 38–41
skills (pupils') 23, 26, 71, 74
PLUS model xi–xiii, 18–19, 169
presentation
IT based 150
oral 146–149
skills 18, 24, 140–1
primary schools 59, 64, 66, 67, 89, 94,
109, 112, 143, 170
pupils
activities 43
behaviour 38, 39, 46–9

discipline 48–9
existing knowledge 67–8, 75, 104,
110
purpose 18, 25, 26, 29, 66–86, 116
communication and 138–9
note taking and 125–7
reading and 111–12

reading 18, 20, 24, 75
for information 108–21
interacting with texts 110–11
note taking and 127–8
purpose and 111–12
strategies 110–12, 125
rejecting 18, 29, 97, 127–8
Reuters 26, 27

scanning 18, 39, 112–17
school librarians
cooperation with teachers   30, 34,
57, 60–4, 170
status of 30, 58, 63, 64
views on information skills 59–60
science 28–9, 62–3, 67, 98
selecting 18, 29, 97, 127–8
self-evaluation 19, 60, 153–64
skimming 18, 39, 112–7
study skills 16, 28, 55, 57, 58, 60, 67

teachers
cooperation with school librarians
30, 34, 51, 60–4, 170
teaching skills 34–53
creating atmosphere 44–6
planning 38–41
delivering lessons 41–4
humour 45–6
thinking skills 18, 25, 67, 75, 138, 166

whole school policies 31, 54–65, 119
World Wide Web 25, 32
writing 137–40, 143–6